IGNACY KRASICKI

THE MOUSEIAD
AND OTHER MOCK EPICS

THE MOUSEIAD AND OTHER MOCK EPICS

by Ignacy Krasicki

Translated from the Polish and introduced by
Charles S. Kraszewski

This book has been published with the support
of the ©POLAND Translation Program

Publishers
Maxim Hodak & Max Mendor

Introduction © 2019, Charles S. Kraszewski

© 2019, Glagoslav Publications

Proofreading by Richard Coombes

www.glagoslav.com

ISBN: 978-1-912894-51-2
ISBN: 978-1-912894-52-9

First published in November 2019

A catalogue record for this book is available from the British Library.

This book is in copyright. No part of this publication may be reproduced, stored in a retrieval system or transmitted in any form or by any means without the prior permission in writing of the publisher, nor be otherwise circulated in any form of binding
or cover other than that in which it is published without a similar condition, including this condition, being imposed
on the subsequent purchaser.

IGNACY KRASICKI

THE MOUSEIAD
AND OTHER MOCK EPICS

Translated from the Polish
and introduced by Charles S. Kraszewski

GLAGOSLAV PUBLICATIONS

Contents

IGNACY KRASICKI:
EIGHTEENTH CENTURY POLAND'S... EVERYTHING 7

THE MOUSEIAD. 41
MONACHOMACHIA OR THE WAR OF THE MONKS. 97
ANTI-MONACHOMACHIA 129
THE CHOCIM WAR. 161

GLOSSARY 233
BIBLIOGRAPHY. 244
ABOUT THE TRANSLATOR. 245

IGNACY KRASICKI

1735 – 1801

INTRODUCTION

Ignacy Krasicki: Eighteenth Century Poland's... Everything

Polish culture is studded with polymaths. From our own days counting backwards, we note Tadeusz Kantor, who revolutionised theatre while also being an important avant-garde painter, and then the giant shoulders he stood upon: Stanisław Wyspiański, dramatist, painter, poet and acolyte of Wagnerian total art, and Stanisław Ignacy Witkiewicz (Witkacy), novelist, dramatist, painter, photographer, and scientist (who researched, on his own person, the effects of psychotropic narcotics on the artistic consciousness. In comparison with them, Ignacy Krasicki is 'merely' a writer. Yet, although he is rarely mentioned in the company of the magnates of the Polish pen, such as Adam Mickiewicz and Jan Kochanowski, he dominates the age in which he flourished like no other. Certainly, Mickiewicz, the national bard of Poland, introduced Romanticism, singlehandedly, to Poland, and created that immense metaphysical theatrical tradition known as Polish Monumental Drama, to which both Wyspiański and Kantor are indebted. Kochanowski, the greatest poet of Poland before Mickiewicz, and the only Renaissance poet of pan-European significance from the Slavic lands, invigorated the stale genre of the lament with his *Threnodies*, translated the Psalter, and created what is arguably the finest humanist tragedy on the Greek model written in the sixteenth century with his *Dismissal of the Grecian Envoys*. Yet neither of them incarnates their age as does Ignacy Krasicki (1735–1801). For this prince of the Church, who served as Primate of Poland from 1795 to 1801, friend and advisor of the last king of Poland and prized acquaintance of that collector of luminaries, Friedrich the Great of Prussia, excelled in all genres of literature typical to the Enlightenment. He is Poland's LaFontaine on account of his *Bajki i przypowieści* [Fables and Parables, 1779-1802], Poland's

Swift, due to his trenchant poetic *Satyry* [Satires, 1779], Poland's Voltaire and Diderot, as the creator of the peripatetic novel in Polish with his *Miłołaja Doświadczyńskiego Przypadki* [The Adventures of Mikołaj Doświadczyński, 1776, the name of whose hero, like Voltaire's 'Candide', is a *nomen omen*, deriving from the Polish word for 'experience' — *doświadczenie*], and Poland's Pope (*Alexander* Pope, that is; the younger son of a magnate clan, he entered the Church more from career concerns than, perhaps, vocation), in his marvellous mock-epics, which form the matter of the present translation. To this constellation of literary excellence we must add his contributions to the budding field of journalism, as a contributing editor to the *Monitor* (1772, much of the content of which were translations and adaptations from the *Spectator*), his work on a two-volume encyclopaedia, and — last but not least — sermons and homiletic writings. Considering the brilliance with which Krasicki excelled in every genre he attempted (save, perhaps, his works for the stage and the less than scintillating serious epic *Chocim War*, also included here), it is difficult to imagine the eighteenth century in Central Europe without him. While there are other important poets of the Neoclassical Age in Poland — Franciszek Karpiński, Adam Naruszewicz and Julian Ursyn Niemcewicz spring to mind — none of them embody the witty *esprit* of the Enlightenment Age as does Krasicki. And nowhere, in Krasicki's writings, is that gorgeously light touch and stinging wit more apparent, than in the mock epics the *Mouseiad* (1775), the *Monachomachia* (1778), and its seeming retraction, the *Anti-Monachomachia* (1780). The late great Slavist and comparatist Harold B. Segel is spot-on when he writes: 'the good bishop's mock-epic poems [...] are the most impressive examples of his literary gifts'.[1]

KRASICKI'S MOCK EPICS

The *Mouseiad* [*Myszeidos*] is often spoken of in the context of the pseudo-Homeric *Batrachomyomachia* [War of the Frogs and Mice], a Hellenistic work dating from the fourth century BC, at

---

[1] Harold B. Segel, Review of Hoisington's translation of *Mikołaj Doświadczyński*, *The Slavic and East European Review*, 38/4 (Winter 1994): 705-706, p. 706.

the earliest, and since classical times ascribed to Homer. Krasicki himself makes a bow of courtesy in this direction in Canto III. But the personification of animals as exemplars of human foibles is an ancient tradition, stretching back to Aesop and through LaFontaine, and, as we mention above, Krasicki was no stranger to this sort of writing, master as he was of the animal fable.

To give just two short examples of this, from his *Fables and Parables,* we offer first 'The Lamb and the Wolves':

> Who seeketh spoil is quick to rationalise.
> Two wolves a straying lamb took by surprise:
> 'You'll eat me?' cried the lamb, 'and by what right?'
> 'Thou'rt tasty, lost, and we've an appetite'.

Krasicki, born in the Royal Republic of Poland in 1735, would turn 60 when his nation was wiped off the map of Europe upon its partitioning between the Empires of Prussia, Russia and Austria. The first of these partitions, when Russia and Prussia carved away chunks of Poland in 1772, saw the See of Warmia, of which Krasicki was then the bishop, torn away from Poland and annexed to Prussia. Although Krasicki's patriotism has been questioned from time to time — mainly due to his friendship with the King of Prussia, to whom, however, he never paid official homage — it is easy to see in these four simple lines his stinging assessment of the 'might makes right' policies which were to lead, eventually, to his nation's disappearance from the political map of Europe, never more to figure on it until 1918.

The reasons for the weakening of the once strong Kingdom of Poland, which was the largest geographical entity in Europe during the Renaissance, and which waged several successful wars against both Muscovy and the Ottoman Empire, are various and murky, and a bit far afield for the introduction to a collection of literary texts. Suffice it to say that there are few black and white hats in history. One man's compromise on behalf of a greater good is treason in the eyes of the idealist. For example, in 1792, a group of Polish nobles, including King Stanisław Poniatowski, rose up, with Russian help, against the reformers who sought to strengthen the nation against future manipulation by their Russian and German neighbours. This is the Targowica Confederacy, named from the city in which it was first organised. Whatever their motives were in turning their weapons against the enlightened Four-Years' Diet of 1791 (which ratified the first modern Constitution in Europe, and the second in the world after the American), Krasicki leaves no doubt as to how he assesses those who act underhandedly, for their own benefit, in the second fable we offer, 'The Heron, the Fish, and the Crab':

> A heron, as the story's told,
> A little blind, and lame, and old,
> Finding himself too slow to catch
> His meal of fish, this plan did hatch:
> He told the fish: 'I've heard something
> Which for you has an evil ring'.
> The fish swam up, and frightened, said:
> 'Speak: of what should we be afraid'?
>
>   'Yesterday,
>   I heard men say
> That it's not really worth the fret
> To fish with hook and line and net:
> "Let's drain the pond, and when it dries,
> We'll march right in and grab the prize".
>
> The panic of the fish was great.
> 'I pity you in your sad state',
> The heron sighed, 'Yet such a woe
> Can be avoided — even so:
> Not far from here's a bubbling creek.
> There will you find the peace you seek.
> Thus, even though the pond be dried,
> You'll frolic yet in the brisk tide'.
> 'So take us there!' the fish implored.
> The heron wavered, hedged, demurred;
> At last, letting himself be swerved,
>   Began to serve.
>
> He picked them up, as if to bear them thence,
> And ate each one behind the fence.

> He thought to fool the crabs with the same news.
> One of them, though, saw through the deadly ruse:
> Perceiving that the heron schemed his wreck,
> He acted swiftly, wrung the villain's neck.
>
> > A belly full, a strangled throat:
> > Traitors take note.

Is the *Mouseiad*, with its plot of a small nation — that of the mice and rats — fighting for its life against the overwhelming odds of larger states — that of the cats, and the reluctant human king Popiel — an allegory of Krasicki's homeland battling bullies abroad and traitors within? Opinion on this point has been divided since the poem first appeared in 1775. For example, whether or not the vicious cat king Mruczysław is to be understood as the overbearing representative of Catherine the Great in Poland, Nikolai Repnin, is unascertainable today. As Krasicki's modern biographer, Tadeusz Dworak, points out, Krasicki subjected the *Mouseiad* to so many revisions, including alterations carried out after King Stanisław had had a chance to read and comment upon the work in manuscript, that it is impossible to find a key that would match all fictional characters, and events, with people and events contemporary to the poet.[2] In his monograph on the poet, Józef Tomasz Pokrzywniak cites Franciszek Ksawery Dmochowski, a contemporary of the poet's, who states that while "'originally written with a satyrical aim in mind, the author later changed his mind and made of it a pure game, entertainment, a joke'. In its present shape, the poem appears to Dmochowski to be "something rather pointless"'[3] [i.e. self-referential, not a comment upon any political reality — CSK].

Of course, the work as it is begs to be pulled apart as some sort of roman-à-clef. Considering the almost anarchic nature of the noble democracy then current in Poland — according to which no decision could be taken in Parliament, however grave, without universal agreement of all members (the so-called 'golden freedom' or *liberum*

---

2   Cf. his 'Discussion on the Allegoric Nature of the *Mouseiad*', Tadeusz Dworak, *Ignacy Krasicki* (Warsaw: Wiedza Powszechna, 1987), pp. 138–168.

3   Józef Tomasz Pokrzywniak, *Ignacy Krasicki* (Poznań: UWM, 2016), p. 68.

veto. A common catchword of the time was *Polska nierządem stoi* [Poland stands by lack of government]) — is it any wonder that Krasicki's depiction of the mice and rats' parliament in Canto II should be taken as a comment upon that Diet debating in Warsaw?

> 'So this is why I've called you here today:
> That you might find some way out of this crisis.
> I'm sure you sense what I don't need to say:
> No time this, for broil 'twixt rats and mice is —
> Your wits united must be put in play.
> For should we fail — I shudder what the price is!
> All rifts now heal, stifle all recrimination —
> At least for now — toil together, for our nation!'
>
> No vain words these, his call for unity;
> For ages, both stirps of the rodent race,
> Though kindred, would flare up in enmity
> From time to time, injuring all estates
> Unto the very loss of liberty.
> Civil unrest undoes the proudest states!
> Only non-rodent foes gain from such spats,
>   When rats quarrel with mice, and mice bicker with rats.

Furthermore, although the poet set his tale in the legendary age of Poland — the story of tyrant King Popiel devoured by mice in his stronghold at Lake Gopło, first related by the mediaeval chronicler Wincenty Kadłubek — is not the drunken dream of the despairing monarch something of a warning to his friend, Stanisław August, about the obligations imposed on him by the trust placed in him by the people?

> Sunk deep in sleep, in dreams before his eyes
> His poisoned forefathers, in sad parade
> — The nation's glory once — gloomily rise,
> In mourning now, who once had been arrayed
> In victors' laurels. Popiel, in such wise
> Pierced with remorse, and with terror half flayed

> That barely he could rule his respiration,
> Must now give ear to their dark denunciation.
>
> (Canto X)

Still, as Dworak points out, referring to the conscious 'blurring' or 'erasure' of whatever allegory may have originally been intended, '[*The Mouseiad* is a] poem, which gives rise to a thousand conjectures, but does not allow for any precise interpretation'.[4] What is most important is that the work does not suffer at all because of this. Rather, true to the eighteenth-century approach to literature, the work is a general comment on the failings and trials common to all humans. Just as in the case of the above-cited fables, in that whatever Polish particulars they may possess, they are understandable to all men to whom injustice and treason are repugnant, so it is with Krasicki's *Mouseiad*. Is it a warning to, or castigation of, the Poles? Sure. But even those who have hardly heard of Poland, to whom Polish history is unknown, can profit by its reading. Krasicki, like Swift and Voltaire and Pope, is a Great European if there ever was one.

Turning to the genre of the mock-epic, which came into full blossom in the so-called 'long' European eighteenth century, it can be most easily described in contrast to the serious epic, which it travesties. Where the epic is lengthy and written in the loftiest poetic style, the mock epic is short — the *Rape of the Lock* is made up of only five short cantos, and while the *Mouseiad* almost reaches the Vergilian twelve books, these too are succinct, and the poetry of the mock epic, far from being lofty, flashes with humour and puns and crisp couplets. Where it does strike an elevated tone, almost always, it does so for reasons of satire. For the epic to be an epic it must have a truly weighty theme. Virgil's *Aeneid* treats of the foundation of Rome; Milton's *Paradise Lost* (and *Regained*), chronicle salvation history. Krasicki's war of cats and mice — why, even the human actors, when urged by King Popiel to set off as a force allied to the cats, rebel in shock at their sovereign's wishes. *Make war against mice? Are you serious?* If the theme of the *Mouseiad*, within the fictional frame of the narrative, is important, it is only so from the perspective of… mice and rats. And here, perhaps, is Krasicki's greatest coup (though none to welcome to Polish ears): greatness and

---

4   Dworak, p. 152.

tragedy are relative. What is a matter of immense significance to us, may seem a minor squabble, an insignificant event in the stream of time, from the perspective of others, or of the ages. Finally, to give one more characteristic of the epic for comparison, we may point out the traditional dual plane of action. In Homer's epics, and that of Virgil — and that of Vyasa in India, for that matter — the trials and triumphs of man on earth are of note to the immortals in the skies, who not only look down upon the action taking place on the human plane, they also enter into the broils as well, on this side or that. In the *Mouseiad*, God is — of course! — entirely absent, as unconcerned about the rat-cat squabble as Voltaire's sultan is about the rats on the ship he sends to Egypt on a trade mission. The 'supernatural' plane is represented by a comic witch, and the traditional journey of the epic hero into the world of wonders is here undertaken by the rat king Gryzomir, who, perforce, sails panicked through the skies, hanging on for dear life behind the hag on her broom. Which, when he comes back down to earth, impresses no one, really; his brother's only response to it is an uneasiness about the murine monarch's seemingly unnatural desire to ally himself with… the bats.

As we note above, Krasicki's writing is universal. People of all national and ethnic backgrounds, of all eras, one would like to say, can enjoy the *Mouseiad* for passages such as this, from Canto III:

> It's not long till Popiel's court comes to know
> How many cats in battle met their doom.
> The chaos and despair steadily grow
> As anguished dames by turns wax wroth and swoon.
> As fur in rage, now hair is torn in woe;
> As blood in streams, now tears and sighs — monsoons!
> The keeners' choir by Princess Duchna's led,
> For Filuś, ah, sweet Filuś! Filuś the cat is dead!
>
> Filuś delightful! Filuś kind and good!
> Filuś who on each couch and bed would laze!
> Filuś of graceful ballerino's foot!
> Filuś who never fasted all his days!
> Filuś abhorred of all the jealous brood
> For how, and on whose breast, he snugly lay!

> But now all that is past, the sun has set
> On faithful Filuś; Duchna has no one to pet.
>
> Eyes that were bright now of their light are spent;
> She weeps, as does the court in sympathy.
> Nought can console her — and so all lament
> Poor Filuś, praising him most mournfully,
> Including more than one tear-sodden gent
> (Who sobs and weeps to mask authentic glee)
> All wring their hands, dig furrows with their knees,
> Preparing for the day of the cat's obsequies.

There is nothing particularly Polish, or even eighteenth-century, in these lines. We all know someone who takes trifles a bit too seriously, and those who play along with that person's whims. Perhaps Krasicki even has us look in the mirror here? Such, as he is to put it in the *Anti-monachomachia*, is the satirist's task: to poke fun in general, 'teaching sweetly', without the meanness of pasquilles, directed at named individuals. There, in Canto III, he writes:

> The weapons of wit can be harmful, snide,
> But helpful too, when they're necessary.
> Behind the jokes, salubrious warnings hide,
> And he, who opts to employ them boldly
> Deserves not to be harshly vilified,
> Oppressed and insulted vengefully!
> Cast off your frenzy, still your mournful moans!
> You too are men: Will you cast the first stones?

And so, in Canto IV of the *Mouseiad*, Krasicki — chronically in debt — fires off a salvo against usurers, without even hinting at the fact that he might actually have some real person in mind. Speaking of the bursting granaries to which the routed mice repair after their thrashing in battle by the cats, he describes them as the property of just such a miser:

> A usurer, for forty years there breeds
> Lucre and gallstones (with his flinty heart),

> Having usurped the land with dodgy deeds,
> Grown rich on toil in which he took no part.
> Believing in no God, he worships greed
> And raises stinginess into an art.
> The heartless dastard, wasted thin with bile,
> Is but the guardian of his unused, useless pile.

Whether or not Krasicki was letting off some steam here, it is one of the few times that the satire takes a bitter, and serious, turn. But in general, the stereotypes he satirises in his mock epics are benign ones. Just as no one would dare suggest that all women are as flighty and moved by trivialities as Princess Duchna described above, after the death of her pet cat, so the satirical depictions of the monks in the *Monachomachia* derive from the stock, sardonic characterisations of religious life in Europe, which no one — and certainly not a Catholic prelate, however 'enlightened' — would suggest is endemic to all tonsured, cowled, and wimpled souls.

Curiously enough, what seems outlandish to our ears — a brawl of monks — is not as freakish as it first appears. During Krasicki's own lifetime, in the reign of August III the Saxon, who proceeded Stanisław Poniatowski on the throne, a quarrel erupted between the Polish and Prussian reformed Franciscans concerning the monastery in Dybów near Toruń. It was referred all the way to Rome, which decided in favour of the Polish monks. However, the Prussians, refusing to acknowledge the decree, 'refused to give over the monastery, appealing to Rome anew. The Polish monks on the other hand, determining to take the monastery by violence if necessary, processed out of Toruń carrying a cross at their head [...] and leading a train of lay people outfitted with clubs ready for the attack and hatchets to chop through the cloister doors...' It ended in minor bloodshed.[5]

Now, the monks we come across in *Monachomachia* are fond of tippling. Invited to have a swig of the needful, Krasicki's scholarly monk reacts as if he'd just been led through a closely-argued syllogism:

> O! Rarely met with, gift of eloquence!
> Who can resist Thy overmastering pow'r?

---

5 Dworak, p. 181, citing Jędrzej Kitowicz.

> To such urgings, the Don had no defence.
> Lifting the cup (in the sweat of his brow)
> He swigged it down — to replenish his strengths;
> Then, to make sure they'd not be flagging now
> (The monks were hanging on his every word),
> He took a second draught, and (just in case) a third.

They are lazy, good-for-nothing, parasites. The hubbub in the cloister, elicited by the spiteful Hag of Discord, penetrates the innermost chambers of the order, where:

> Father Hilary, awakened by the sound,
> Bearishly vexed, grumbled, 'What's going on!?'
> The Prior, too, blinking from bed of down,
> For the first time in years beheld the dawn.
> The thickest cushion availed not to drown
> The frightful din; so soon the cloister Don
> — Damning too-healthy ears — in angry haste
> Left book and bed, and into refectory raced.

This theme, along with that of their fondness for drink, most characterises the monks in Krasicki's poem. In Canto II of the *Mouseiad,* the rat-king Gryzomir's court is centred in the main hall of a monastery. Intended by its founder for a library, it has been converted into an opulent larder. In the *Monachomachia*, here too books are forgotten things. Challenged to a dispute by a rival order, Krasicki's heroes must set out on a heroic quest (another epic characteristic!) in search of that strange implement:

> 'Thus, we must hit the books. Now, ancient lore,
> Passed down by generations of our kind,
> Declares that, somewhere, we've a hefty store
> Of books, patiently waiting for the time
> Someone shall crack them open. It's been more
> Than thirty years since Alphonse had a mind
> To broach the — what d'you call it? — library
> Up in the rafters; it's high time we go and see

> 'What's to be found there; perhaps something of use?
> Even the slightest bucklers can protect'.
> He spoke, but all fell silent. Each refused
> To undertake the hazards of the trek;
> Each had a fitting, readymade excuse
> To shun the deed. At last the monks elect
> Two gentle, backward souls to search the nooks
> And crannies for those fabled creatures known as — books.

This is all good fun. The closest that Krasicki comes to a rationalist — nearly Protestant — scathing of the cloistered orders is when he mocks them for being superstitious. On the very day when the envoys of the challenging abbey are to appear at his monastery's door, Fr Raymund, hastening to the cloister gate to gossip with the locale *devotes*, stumbles and falls to the ground. This, as he explains to his friend Fr Rafał, bending over him in concern, is a bad sign:

> 'Alas, my friend! In misfortune begun,
> Unlucky will unfold this fatal day!
> "The first step sets the paths the planets run"
> Is what I've heard the wisest prophets say.
> Nothing can change what Destiny has spun —
> I rose, I ran, I fell — and here I lay!
> An evil sign — catastrophe awaits!
> Today's no day for gossip at the dear cloister gates!'

Quite un-Christian, and irrational, the faith that the monk places in astrology and predestination: Diderot's *grand rouleau d'en haut*. But is the satire here directed at the superstition of the monk (which appears only here, for comic effect), or his old-womanish interest in chewing the local fat at the cloister gate (when perhaps he should be at his books, or in the chancel stalls singing the hours? No *ora et labora* type he!) No, Krasicki is far from suggesting that all monks are like this; no more than he would suggest that every comely woman with a prayerbook is a religious hypocrite, such as he — seems to — characterise the Vicegerent's wife in Canto IV:

Now, she'd a figure full of grace; her eyes,
Half-closed in prayer, at times would flash with flame;
A fetching lisp (although her words were pious),
Dressed modestly (yet such a minxy frame
Reveals itself to each who barely tries
His fancy) in short: she'd mastered the game.
The while she fingered her beads, piously humming,
Hyacinth mused of a different second coming.

'Twas not with thin romances that she fed her
Sweet intellect, not vampire, ghoul, nor wraith;
She read Erasmus, discoursed on d'Agreda
(Her Gothic was pure, of the Age of Faith.)
To hear her scourge sin, you'd have thought her dead, or
Cold to delight, but then, in the next breath,
You caught a… soupçon… of impropriety;
The way she teased, she'd slay a man with piety.

Krasicki is a satirist, but not a scornful mocker. If he deals some smarting blows, they are not directed at women, or monks, or religious life per se (as the righteously incensed monks of the *Antimonachomachia* would label the author of the *Monachomachia*), but rather at the abuses of the same. And again we are reminded of the *Fables*, so similar in tone, and purpose, to these mock epics. Take 'The Pharisee', for example:

> The maid her mistress piqued exactly when
> That pious woman's prayers were at an end.
> Spinning round, in anger her features set,
> And finishing her plea: 'Forgive our debts
> As we *our* debtors,' she thumped, walloped, beat.
> Lord, may Thy justice ever be as meet.

Writing in the *Slavic and East European Review*, Wanda Dźwigała notes:

> Granted, Krasicki fought persistently to bring Enlightenment thought to Polish society. Yet to search for deeper similarities, especially in the religious views of Voltaire and Krasicki, would

be misleading. The Polish poet's satires were never as malicious nor as devastating as were Voltaire's attacks on established institutions in France. Moreover, the purpose of *Monachomachia* was to attack scholasticism and satirise the superstitions, ignorance, gluttony, drunkenness and laziness which prevailed in those religious orders in Poland which had not experienced the influence of Enlightenment thought. Krasicki's satire was witty, not insulting or brutal, nor was it as harsh and sarcastic as Voltaire's attacks on the Church. And most significantly, Krasicki's mockery was designed to improve the clergy, while Voltaire's attacks were designed to destroy the clergy.[6]

But people of his time — and some time after — were not willing to see things this way. According to Dmochowski, *Monachomachia* first saw the light of day in Sans-Souci, where 'Friedrich II gave the author that same apartment in the Sans-Souci palace in which Voltaire had stayed, telling him that in such a place he ought to feel inspired, and write something beautiful'.[7] This was enough to raise a red flag for Stanisław Tarnowski. Writing over one hundred years after the original publication of the *War of the Monks*, he considered the satirical poem as little less than an act of treason:

> There are two reasons why we can't quite hold [*Monachomachia*] in respect. First of all, it cannot be doubted that, if there were bad monasteries, backward monasteries, lazy and full of drunkenness, it was the bishop's job to punish and reform them — but not to mock them. And if it wasn't proper for the bishop to stand on the side of the *philosophes* against the regular orders, all the more so was it not proper for a Pole, after the partitions, to do anything to please and delight old Friedrich.[8]

It was in answer to such criticism — in belated answer, for published four years after the first poem — that Krasicki brought out his

---

6 Wanda Dzwigala, 'Voltaire and the Polish Enlightenment: Religious Responses', *The Slavic and East European Review* 81/1 (January 2003):70-87, p. 77.

7 Quoted by Pokrzywnia, p. 69.

8 Tarnowski, vol. III, p. 266.

'retraction' of the work, the humorously entitled *Anti-Monachomachia*. That he was not over-troubled by the attacks on his person following the *War of the Monks* can be seen in the general tenor of the retraction:

> Sloth had no place in this monastery
> Wherein she tried to sow her tragic seed;
> Here was the pattern of integrity —
> A cloister wide-famed for heroic deed,
> The choice of all who sought true sanctity,
> A granary of faith, where all did feed.
> Blessed exemplar! Too feeble is my song
> To hymn your praise aright, O fortress true, and strong!

Methinks the poet doth protest too much. As Czesław Miłosz puts it, 'he seemingly retracts his insinuations, but is even more malicious in his irony'.[9] Indeed, if the foibles of the monks in *Monachomachia* are grotesque, unbelievable, so the virtues of the monks presented in *Anti-Monachomachia* are just as transparently comic. In the new work, Krasicki does little more than assert, as above, the piety and wisdom and goodness of the tonsured brethren — many of whom are the same, or at least share the same names — as the monks in the previous work, and the careful reader is quick to realise that this too is part of his comic strategy. It is a false retraction, because he has nothing to retract. The over exaggerated vices of *Monachomachia* find a bookending over-exaggeration of virtue in *Anti-Monachomachia,* and in this Krasicki's deep humanism shines forth. Nor here, nor there is the truth of humanity in general, or religious life in particular, but in the grey, human shades that lie between them. It is an eminently rational argument, *philosophes* or no *philosophes*. As Dworak puts it:

> The praise [heaped on the cloister in this work] doesn't come off as all that convincing. Firstly, because this ideal of a monastery must arouse suspicion — no such monastery was known of in Poland. Secondly, we have here a simple rhetorical contradiction of the opinion expressed in the *Monachomachia*.

---

9   Czesław Milosz, *History of Polish Literature* (Berkeley: California, 1983), p. 178.

> The caricature of a monastery there is contrasted with a monastery-Utopia here, as if the poet were asking: judge for yourselves which of the two is closer to the truth.[10]

There is great, subtle, comedy in the *Anti-Monachomachia*. If it has one flaw, it is that it cannot be properly understood unless one reads it in tandem with the earlier work. Unless one has already met Brother Hyacinth,

> Of cloistered sisters the great favourite
> (Excepting Rafał), slim, of great beauty,
> His cowl — ah, wanton winds toyed with it
> As through the sacred halls on dancer's foot he
> Glided;

and read through the tantalising scene in Canto IV of *Monachomachia* where Hyacinth, adverse to all fisticuffs, is closeted with the flirty wife of the Vicegerent, one misses the joke entirely in Canto IV of the *Anti-Monachomachia*, where his penchant for dallying with the fair sex — which we have just witnessed! — is overthrown with the simple denial of his being interested in anything other than books. Speaking of the Vicegerent's wife, who sometimes receives the prior, chastely accompanied by another monk, on visits, the poet states:

> Hyacinth of such favour never tasted.
> No one frequented her, except the prior,
> But whether he did or no, he always fasted.
> And if he took along with him some friar,
> Such visits Hyacinth would deem as wasted.
> For vain and vulgar, earthly, he thought all
> Corporal delight; he tended book, not bottle.

So, which is it? Monks are lazy, drunken, hypocritical womanisers? Or pious, studious celibate heroes of the cloistered life? The truth, again, lies somewhere between the two extremes. And, as Krasicki points out to his detractors in the *Anti-Monachomachia*, the very point of

---

10   Dworak, p. 202.

satire, like the comedy of humours so popularised by Ben Jonson and Molière, is to paint an impersonal, but striking portrait of a human vice. If any individual feel the lash across his or her back, it can only be because they see themselves, like it or not, in the personified trait. As we see in the conversation between the monastery librarian and Father Honoratus, when the latter is moved to the core by what he takes to be a personal attack upon himself, and monastic life in general:

> 'But he attacked me!' 'Mere coincidence!'
> 'Coincidence? He mocked my advanced years!'
> 'In person? I suppose there's a slight chance.
> But had he you in mind? That's far from clear.
> How have we been defamed, good Father, since
> What he expressed — It didn't happen here!
> Such witty sallies no man ever minds
> Unless… within himself, a grain of truth he finds.
>
> 'Mere hazard, that he chanced to use your name.
> His Honoratus isn't him we know.
> Are you as stubborn as an ass gone lame?
> Which brother finds in you a bitter foe?
> Who calls you lazy? Who has ever blamed
> You for a drunk, to books and matins slow?
> You're good! You're wise! Prone to divine afflatus!
> That screed's nothing to do with our Honoratus!'

Whether or not, as the poet states, tongue in cheek, the *Monachomachia* should have been better hidden, so that the Hag of Discord should not find it,[11] and pervert its meaning to her own nefarious ends, it is certainly true that those who are scandalised by its lecture are being led astray by something that is not to be found in the poetry itself. Witness the scene in Father Gaudenty's cell, where the otherwise peaceful (!)

---

11 Before he had the chance to bring it out in Warsaw himself, a copy of the text, obtained who knows where, was rumoured to be on the presses at Königsberg. Krasicki swiftly wrote to the authorities there, ascribing the authorship to his secretary, and demanding that any copies already printed be confiscated. See Dworak, p. 173 *ff.*

monk is aroused to battle by the Hag of Discord, appearing to him in the guise of Religion:

> 'You sleep, my knight, while all the rest are waking?
> You're at your ease, while all your brothers weep?
> Are you so lazy, selfishly forsaking
> Me, and the common weal, in languorous sleep?
> Arise! Your mother's heart would you be breaking?
> Ingrate, her honour thus to rate so cheap!
> Arise and help, if you've a beating heart!
> If you're no bastard child, arise! And do your part!'
>
> Had she not vanished as quick as she came,
> She'd've caught herself a smart blow on the ear,
> So quick the kindling of his soul took flame,
> And he leapt from his cot, anger and fear
> Racing with pity through his every vein,
> So zealous to avenge his order dear.
> But out the window, up into the sky
> The peevish hag flew, sounding the dire battlecry.

Here we have one of the most brilliant epic mirrorings in the mock epics of Ignacy Krasicki. Those familiar with Virgil's *Aeneid* immediately recognise the allusion to that scene when Turnus is approached by the Fury, who first seeks to convince him, in the guise of a familiar, pious woman from the temple, to rise up in arms against the newcomers from Troy. But then, when he responds — quite rationally — that he'll take what she says under consideration, but won't rush off to act before he determines what is best for him and his nation, she uncovers her true self, plunges a firebrand into his breast, and effectively possesses him with the misguided rage against Aeneas that will lead him to his death. Had he remained in possession of his faculties, most likely, there would have been no war over Lavinia. Here too, the fury over *Monachomachia* is shown as an artificial thing — a suspension of reason in those who indulge in it. It is an elegant little allusion, and meaningful. Krasicki does not deserve the belittling he receives at the hands of Stanisław Tarnowski, who sums up the genre of the eighteenth-century mock epic, including the *Mouseiad, Monachomachia,* and *Anti-Monachomachia,* in such deprecating terms:

> In just such times when poetic creativity had begun to dry up in Europe, it was natural that such a false and tasteless genre should begin to take root. People, who hadn't the requisite talent to compose truly heroic epics, promised themselves fame, success, adulation or money via the composition of parodies, aping heroic forms, in which they consciously set the most trivial and comical themes. The resulting contradiction, unbearable to us, was intended to have a comic effect, and indeed, as it was, it pleased the readers of the time.[12]

It has been said that one needs to be an adult in order to appreciate the literature of the Enlightenment period. Perhaps one must also retain enough of the playful attitude of the child, or, maybe, certain eras produce people who are *too* mature, like Tarnowski, to appreciate the innocuous rough-and-tumble game of satire. At any rate, I feel confident that, whatever the tastes of Europeans circa 1905 may have been, in the subsequent 100+ years that have passed since Tarnowski brought out his great *History of Polish Literature,* we have regained enough of our youth, or our humour, to find mock-epics such as Krasicki's three great comedies more than bearable.

In his book on Krasicki, the French scholar Paul Cazin notes: 'The *Mouseiad* is still read today. Its style retains its charm. Never before had the Polish muse expressed herself with such limpidity and ease, with so elegant a simplicity'.[13] One agrees wholeheartedly with this statement. Nowhere else, save perhaps in the *Fables and Parables,* is Krasicki's witty, light and comic poetic genius on such evident display as it is in the three mock-epics. He is on firm ground here. It is only when he feels the need to try his strengths at the straight, serious, Virgilian epic, that he comes up short.

---

12   Tarnowski, vol. III, p. 265.
13   Paul Cazin, *Le prince-évêque de Varmie, Ignace Krasicki* (Paris: Bibliothèque polonaise, 1940), p. 106.

THE *CHOCIM WAR*

The *Chocim War* (1780) is Ignacy Krasicki's one attempt at the serious epic. It is not the only Polish epic on the topic of the defence of Chocim against the Ottoman Turks in 1621. As a matter of fact, when the title *Wojna chocimska* is brought up in discussions amongst Poles, it is not Krasicki's work that springs to mind, but rather the much earlier *Transakcja Wojna Chocimskiej* of Wacław Potocki, published in 1670. In his critical overview of Krasicki's works, Tadeusz Dworak places the *Chocim War* amongst the *utwory mniejszego znaczenia* ('works of lesser significance') of the poet.[14]

The fact that two full-length epics have been written about the Chocim conflict is not as surprising as the fact that any should have been written at all. Although often described as a Polish victory, the three-week-long siege of Chocim was more of a stalemate than a ringing success of Polish arms. While it did avenge the Polish rout at the battle of Cecora — referenced by Krasicki — and firm up the southeastern border of the Polish Commonwealth, negating Ottoman pretensions to the subjugation of Poland and enjoining upon the Porte a policy of peaceful relations with Poland through the border-areas of Moldova it controlled, the Chocim battle really only reaffirmed the *status quo ante bellum*. Now, I do not wish to diminish the heroism or sacrifice of the Poles and their allies battling at Chocim. I am speaking here purely from a literary perspective. For, if one wishes to have a go at the composition of a serious, national, military epic, why choose Chocim and not the truly heroic, indisputably victorious, lifting of the siege of Vienna by Jan III Sobieski? The routing of the Turks at Vienna by the Polish hussars under the command of King Jan is perhaps the most significant, greatest pan-European triumph of Polish arms that ever was. To employ a risky metaphor, which will probably anger some and certainly date me, why ask the thrice-divorced, overweight welfare mother next door out on a date, when Brigitte Bardot has been dropping hints right and left, begging your friends and acquaintances for your phone number? As far as Potocki is concerned, the Lifting of the Siege at Vienna — an epic victory of the same significance for European culture as that of Charles Martel at Poitiers — was still thirteen years in the offing when he decided to write his epic. But

---

14 See Dworak, pp. 460–479.

Krasicki? It was almost a full century after the fact when, as part of his propaganda battle to swing the Russian Empire into an alliance against the Turks, King Stanisław August commissioned the epic from his friend, the poet-bishop.[15] Was the choice of theme determined by the King? If so, that would let Krasicki — who makes a courteous nod in the direction of Sobieski's future glories in the epic — off the hook. If not, well, the mind is boggled. Sobieski and Vienna had to wait another one hundred years before a writer took the story in hand — until 1878, when the novelist Józef Ignacy Kraszewski brought out his *Pamiętnik Mroczka* [Diary of Mroczek].

Krasicki's *Chocim War* is not a masterpiece. It comes off poorly even in comparison with Potocki's work. Tarnowski calls it Krasicki's 'weakest' poetic work; that may be so, but it is still eminently readable, and as a work of Krasicki's pen, it simply cannot be ignored. However, it is difficult not to agree, at least partially, with the Cracovian critic's assessment of the work, that in it, Krasicki shows no 'creative fantasy; his characters are neither fleshed out nor alive, nor does the poem have any vibrant epic action,' or that the scenes when the guardian angel of Poland appears before the throne of the Almighty in order to beg His protection for the Poles was 'well thought-out, but needed the genius of a Milton' — which, we are to understand, Krasicki did not possess. He then proceeds to a brave attempt at saying something nice about a poet he admires, in the end, but all he can come up with is surely the greatest left-handed compliment ever offered a writer by a critic:

> In general, one can say about the poem that it is cool, horizontal, but honest. It's not capable of firing anyone with enthusiasm. Even its contemporaries though it weak, but it contains no great errors of composition, nor grand tonal disharmonies, or improbabilities. Its one error, and it is a cardinal error in a narrative poem, arising in this case from the author's innate lack of imagination, is that his figures have no life of their own, his scenes no movement; nothing stands out or strikes the reader, nothing speaks to his imagination or his feelings; everything is uniformly colourless and correct, pale and cloying. The entirety of the poem gives one the impression of something created by a

---

15 Dworak, p. 460.

man who had no talent whatsoever, but was a reasonable man nonetheless; a person who could create nothing grand, but was able to fulfil his task in such a way that he comes away from it without having become a laughingstock.¹⁶

Well.

Tarnowski goes on to compare Krasicki's *Chocim War* with that of Potocki — to the latter's advantage — but there's no need to continue. It is enough to say that the *Chocim War* is an interesting text, as a serious epic, in comparison with the mock-epic masterpieces such as the *Mouseiad* and the *Monachomachia*, which is the very reason we include it in our book. Granted, such a work seems not 'innate' to Krasicki, whose genius is comic, not tragic, a biting wit, not given to flights of the sublime. Harold Lloyd and Stan Laurel are geniuses in their own genres — but no one would ever think of casting them as Hamlet. That said, just as Virgil's *Aeneid*, no less a work commissioned for purposes of propaganda, tells us how the Romans wished to be thought of, so in Krasicki's *Chocim War* may we find an interesting mirror for how the Poland of his age — and perhaps not only — wished to present itself to the world at large.

Above all then is the trope of 'Poland, the bulwark of Christianity'. Because of its once great size (at its height, the Polish-Lithuanian Commonwealth stretched from the Baltic to the Black Sea), Catholic Poland was in constant contact, and frequent conflict, with the Islamic empire of the Ottoman Turks. The idea of Poland as the bastion of Christian Europe, protecting Christendom from the expansionist onslaught of the Turks, is an old one. Perhaps the greatest expression of this idea is to be found in the poems of the seventeenth-century neo-Latin poet, Maciej Kazimierz Sarbiewski, known and widely-read throughout Latin Europe as Sarbievius. In his poetry, the Jesuit often castigates the quarrelling nations of Europe, especially those

---

16   Tarnowski, vol. III, pp. 336, 337, 338. Dmocbowski was a little more understanding in this regard. Although he considered the *Chocim War* 'rather a bit of history written in verse [than an epic in its own right], with a few fictional passages as decoration', he still applauded the effort: 'To fall short in a great endeavour is not without its glory. The genius of man has striven for three thousand years now to create that "divine work", with only three succeeding: Homer, Vergil and Tasso'. Cited in Pokrzywniak, p. 69.

who have fallen out in armed conflict over the Catholic/Protestant divide, chastising them like some modern Lysistrata for being brothers worshipping at the same altar who still will not unite their strengths against the true threat: the Muslim Turk. The threat posed by the Ottomans is enunciated by Krasicki in Canto I of his epic, where the Sultan, determined upon 'exterminating' the Christian nations, is encouraged by his advisors to:

> Spread wide throughout the world [Muhammed's] holy writ.
> In slavery we shall the stubborn yoke;
> While to the pliable we shall mercy show.
> The farthest lands shall know our victory;
> All men shall hear our all-triumphant cries,
> And Rome, that once held pride of place before
> All nations, shall now kneel to Istanbul.

The significance of Chocim, then, is in this trope of 'Poland, Bulwark of Christendom', as the nearby city of Kamieniec in the Ukraine is described thus:

> This is the fatal flaw in the bold pagan's
> Plans: this fortress of the fatherland, redoubt
> Of Christendom.

And so, not conquest, not even elimination of a threat, is what the Poles are after, but showing to the world again that they are the defensive walls of Europe, behind which the Christian nations can sleep securely. It is almost as if Krasicki *opts* for Chocim over Vienna here. For the latter exploit, while saving Vienna from the Turkish yoke and bringing Islamic expansionism to a halt, did not remove the threat, it only set it in abeyance. It would be false, therefore, to overemphasise the Polish victory at the foot of the Kahlenberg. Chocim, on the other hand, delivers a more modest, but all the more realistic and secure promise. The Turks aren't going anywhere, Krasicki seems to suggest. The threat will always be there. But Poland will always remain what it always has been: the firm breastwork against which the Turkish flood will beat in vain, always to recede.

To best understand Krasicki's *Chocim War*, the proper context for the work is not the Virgilian epic tradition, but rather that of the *chanson de geste*, of which the mediaeval *Chanson de Roland* is the flagship. In that patriotic retelling of the fateful retreat of Charlemagne through the Spanish Pyrenees, the battle of the Christian French and the 'pagan' Moors is shown in garish contrast. Near the end of laisse LXXIX, we read the bald statement that sounds like a battlecry: *Paien unt tort e christiens unt dreit!* 'The Pagans are wrong, and the Christians are right!' You can't get a much clearer idea of the poet's opinion than that. In the *Chanson de Roland* there is no middle ground, no subtle shading, no consideration of the 'other' as a human being such as we find in the near-contemporary *Cantar de mio Cid*, in which Christians are sometimes shown as the fiercest enemies of the most Catholic hero Ruy Díaz, and at least one Muslim — Abengalbón — is painted in noble, heroic colours, as a friend and supporter of the Cid. For the author of the *Chanson de Roland*, the Muslims are always *félons* and *traitres*. Similarly, in Krasicki's work, the fundamental difference between Christian Pole and Muslim Turk can be seen even in their motivation: 'The infidels with wildness brave, the Poles / By honour urged, emboldened by virtue', he describes the fight in Canto V. Nothing changes in this regard by Canto XI, near the end of the work: 'On this side Faith made warriors strong; on that: / A spiteful hatred made the faithless bold'. Examples of Krasicki's description of Islam as a barbarous, 'faithless' creed might be multiplied at will. Suffice it to say that, however true it may have been of him that he 'believed natural religion to be in accord with that most human of attributes, Reason [and that] he had words of praise for all religions',[17] that is certainly not the case here! Indeed, 'Truly, in the *Chocim War* Krasicki concentrates his Christian worldview to a maximum degree, in comparison to the rest of this works'.[18]

Likewise, the Poles are shown as loyal, obeying the rulers that God has set over them, out of love. In Canto V, the poet interjects:

> Our fathers always were eager to show
> The love they bore the ruling dynasty;
> Though equal to his majesty in law,
> Poles always cherish the blood of their kings.

---

17 Miłosz, p. 176.

18 Dworak, p. 468.

The Turks, on the other hand, obey their ruler Osman slavishly, out of fear: 'All came at once, at his command, so great / They feared the Turkish tyrant to displease', he writes in Canto VIII. The only real exception to this rule is the Turkish hero Skinder. When, in Canto XII, the now twice defeated Osman determines to capitulate and seek terms from the victorious Poles, Skinder erupts with disdainful anger:

> 'O, you sordid mob!'
> [...] 'grovelling in defeat —
> The scum that barely crept into the light
> From caverns where our mighty arms had chased them
> Are now rejoicing in their victory?
> And you would pray? The manly spirit seeks
> Revenge when checked! Strong arms, not pliant knees!
> O, who is used to triumph rushes out
> Onto a path that leads to victory,
> Or noble death!'

Indeed, of all the speeches Krasicki sets in the mouths of his protagonists, Skinder's final words are the most memorable, the most heartfelt and genuine. Krasicki ennobles the proud pagan by showing him to be a different kind of creature from his servile compatriots. In his anger at being chosen as one of the envoys to beg peace at the Polish camp, he hesitates not to brashly cast his disdain in the teeth of Osman himself:

> 'Let him who first encroached against the laws
> Of man, himself be on his way to fix them!
> Let him, whose feet erred from Submission's path
> Go face his shameful sentence! He, who would
> Add shame to shame by treading honour prone!
> There must be some devoid of honour here
> Who'll take no taint from cringing in the dust!
> Let such go!'

But such an exotic flower simply can't grow in the poisoned soil of the Turkish camp. At this very moment, the disillusioned and infuriated

Skinder plunges his sword into his own heart — and truly sets the seal upon the Turkish defeat.

Of course, it had to end this way for him; God is on the side of the Christian Poles. Even in the early cantos, like Canto II, where the sudden onslaught of the Turks at the Polish border causes panic, the poet is quick to calm the fluttering hearts with an assurance that might be underscored as the main thrust of his poem:

> The trembling people flee for sanctuaries
> Which fill with earnest prayers and floods of tears;
> Women and children sobbing, congregation
> And priest beg the Lord God to turn aside
> His anger. Aid eternal: from fierce hands
> The weak You do deliver, from harsh fate;
> For Fate is in Your hands. You raise the fallen —
> This you have taught us often, and confirmed.
> Look down upon these wretched pale figures!
> To whom will You abandon them as prey?
> For You have promised, though the day seem lost —
> No one has ever perished trusting You.

Which brings us to one of the more interesting leitmotifs of Krasicki's epic: his insistence upon predestination. At Chodkiewicz's wedding, when the news of his commission arrives, the poet notes:

> It was not destiny caused this, but He
> Who holds fate in His hand. Almighty God,
> Directing all, governing all.

This is the tenor of the work throughout. We are not even tantalised, as Homer tantalises us, when his Zeus holds up the golden scales of fate during the crucial battle between Achilles and Hector. As Krasicki remarks in Canto X: 'all unfolds according to His plan — / Neither coincidence nor chance exists'. This is a very bold statement, considering that Christian theology traditionally emphasises man's free will. God, while foreseeing all, does not cause everything to happen. The idea of a world in which all plays out according to an immutable plan carved in stone, as it were, by God, is more characteristic of Islam, the religion of the Poles' enemies. However, at nearly each juncture where the trope of Fate being determined by God is mentioned, what follows is the Christian hero's acceptance of his duty. That is where the emphasis of Krasicki's text really lies: the noble Christian hero, accepting adversity and difficult obligations out of pious devotion to God. Again, this is what marks Islam, which word means, in fact "submission." However, with the Christian background of free will, taken for granted by Krasicki as always in the reader's mind (Chodkiewicz and the others could refuse to do what they know God wants them to do, after all), the Poles are shown to be even more pious and duty-bound than their enemies, who thus describe the entirety of their religious experience.

Perhaps the same thing can be said for Ignacy Krasicki. Like his hero Chodkiewicz, the illustrious old campaigner, whose walls are hung with the trophies of stunning past victories, so Krasicki, the greatest satirical poet born on Polish soil, obeys the King and rushes off into the field to win new laurels in the perilous genre of the epic. Did he obtain them? Tarnowski would say, No, but at least he gave no ground. He battled on to a respectable stalemate.

Or perhaps something more. The great thing about art is that it is constantly present. Whatever the case might have been in the eighteenth century, the nineteenth or the early twentieth century, Krasicki is able to take the field again, with You, Reader, as his new arbiter — today's crown of bay is in your hand now, to dispose of, as you wish.

THE PRESENT TRANSLATIONS

As a translator, I feel it incumbent upon myself to bring over into English, not only the ideological content of the original, but also its form. My translations of Adam Mickiewicz's *Forefathers' Eve* and the plays of Juliusz Słowacki and Stanisław Wyspiański are rhymed, simply because these poets decided on what the Poles call *mowa wiązana* [linked speech] for their poetic expression, and I am convinced that not to respect their formal choices, would be just as treacherous as playing fast and loose with the thoughts they express. This translation of Ignacy Krasicki's heroic and mock-heroic verse is no different, or, if it is, only slightly, and I believe justifiably so, as I explain below.

The four works collected in this book were all originally composed in *ottava rima*, the preferred verse form of Tasso (*Orlando Furioso*) — Krasicki's favourite poet.[19] The rhyme scheme is ABABABCC. Krasicki's stanza consists of eight lines, each of which is eleven syllables long — one of the classical verse lines of Polish prosody, the other being a line of thirteen syllables. I have reproduced the *Mouseiad,* the *Monachomachia* and the *Anti-Monachomachia* in this stanza form. The only departure from this being the adoption of the five-foot, mostly iambic, line familiar to the English ear, and the lengthening, à la Spenser, of the concluding line of each stanza from five to six feet.

This is a magnificent form for the light touch, punning, and snappy wit for which the mock-epics of the eighteenth century are renowned. For this very reason it was chosen by Lord Byron for his masterpiece *Don Juan*. It is less well fitting, in my opinion, for the stately atmosphere of the serious, heroic epic. On the one hand, ever since Milton, at least, the English ear expects heroic narratives to be composed in blank verse. The first few lines signal to the reader that the joking is over; we're now rolling up our sleeves to get down to serious business. On the other hand, the obligation of rhyme, and especially the concluding couplets, can lead in English to a Rococo levity, not to say a limerick-like bounciness, both of which are completely foreign to the heroic genre, and do violence to the exalted theme of the work.

For these two reasons, I have departed from my usual practice of reproducing the verse form of the original *Chocim War* as closely as possible. Paradoxically, this departure may result in Krasicki's one epic sounding more natural in its English version.

The conscious decision to abandon rhyme and eschew the stanza form in favour of the more familiar Miltonic iambic pentameter led to one unexpected advantage, which I hope the reader will appreciate. The varying poetic quality of Krasicki's one venture into heroic verse has already been noted. I will point out just one more compositional flaw, which has a direct bearing on the subject at hand: Repetitiveness. One of the great characteristics of the classical epic is the extended metaphor. Vergil, of course, is the great master of this; his extended metaphor of 'duty-bound' Aeneas as an Alpine oak, buffeted by the winds and made to sway, yet never uprooted from his grounding in

---

19 Dworak, p. 132.

what he knows to be right, is the most famous of them all. If, as some have said, Krasicki lacks imagination in the *Chocim War*, nowhere is that more visible than here. Nearly all of Krasicki's metaphors are drawn from nature, and nearly all of these, in turn, from atmospheric phenomena: approaching storms, lightning bolts, fields of wheat bent beneath the raging gale. Such metaphors appear with such numbing regularity throughout the poem, that one almost wonders if the poet had read his work over before submitting it to print. Had he done so, by the third repetition of 'Just as the storm clouds, swelling over fields…' he might well have said *Hold on, I've overused that one, I reckon. Perhaps we'll describe the approaching army in another way?* As far as such repetition is concerned, there was nothing to do about it. They have been reproduced faithfully, and if the reader has had enough of them by the fourth go round, blame Krasicki, not me.

The real problem with repetitiveness in the *Chocim War* is directly the result of the stanza form chosen by the poet. Once Krasicki determined on following Tasso and composing his epic in *ottava rima*, he was obligated to fill out all eight lines — and sometimes, he didn't have enough batter, so to speak, to fill all the depressions in the baking pan. The result was a watering down of the batter, to continue with our metaphor; saying in eight lines — as the chosen form dictated — something that could be just as well, or better, said in three. After all, the great defining characteristic of verse, that which gives poetry its power, is economy of speech. By deciding to translate the *Chocim War* into blank verse, we freed ourselves from the tyranny of the stanza, and were able to cut out a good deal of the fat with which Krasicki was obliged to lard his pan. For one example, consider the following twenty four lines from Canto X. Here, the soul of Władysław Warneńczyk is giving Chodkiewicz a lesson in astronomy:

>   Patrz, jakim lotem dzielnie poruszone
>   Kolei trzymając w swym biegu stateczną,
>   W obrębach swoich gwiazdy umieszczone,
>   Idą w krąg, w podłuż, lub drogą poprzeczną.
>   Patrz, jako dalej ledwo postrzeżone,
>   W tej, co wy drogą nazywacie mleczną,
>   Każda do swojej zmierzająca mety,
>   Są niezliczone słońca i planety.

Kunszt wasz przemyślny temu nie poradził,
Czemu dostarczyć wzrok tępy nie zdoła:
Co Bóg nad wami w niebiosach osadził,
Widzicie postać, jak świetna, wesoła.
Słońc, planet, światów niezmierność zgromadził,
Lecz wam ukryte ich zwroty i koła.
Zmyślność, co nadal rzeczy nie dościga,
Widzi światełko mdłe, które się miga.

Wszystkie ogółem, i każde osobne,
Częścią są istną niezmiernego wątku:
Każde do skutków właściwych sposobne,
Na to zdziałane z samego początku,
Ażeby wzajem wspaniałe, ozdobne,
Do powszechnego zmierzały porządku;
A jawnem piętnem rządu przedziwnego,
Głosiły wielkość stworzyciela swego.

In an English prose-trot, these lines read:

Look, with what flight bravely moved,
Keeping their place in the stately march,
The stars, set in their own limits,
Move in circles, lengthwise, or parallel.
Look further, how barely noticed,
In that, which you call the Milky Way,
Each one moves toward its own goal —
Innumerable, the suns and planets.

Your clever art is not equal to this,
What your dull sight can barely reveal:
What God has set above you in the heavens:
You see the figure, how glorious, how gay.
He has gathered together innumerable suns and planets,
But their turns and circles are hidden from you.
Physical sense, which still cannot capture these things
Only sees a pale little light, blinking.

> Everything together, and each one by itself,
> Forms an essential part of the measureless weft:
> Each fashioned to its own ends,
> From the very beginning created for that action,
> So that together, splendid, festive,
> They should contribute to the universal order,
> And with the visible seal of this awesome, mysterious order,
> Proclaim the greatness of their creator.

Fairly windy that. It takes Krasicki twenty-four lines to say:

> The glory of the heavens, barely perceptible to the human eye,
> In which each part moves in harmony with the others
> Creates an awesome, complicated, dance-like pattern
> Which from the very beginning, testifies to the greatness
>   of its creator?

There's a lot of repetition in these lines, *forced* repetition, one would say, imposed upon the poet by his choice of a regular stanza form that has to be filled out. Our rendition of these three stanzas reduces the twenty-four lines to eighteen:

> Behold the orbits of the stars of Heaven.
> Each in its predetermined arcs and sines
> Rolling majestically, ellipse and vector,
> See how each star and planet in that cloud
> Of worlds you mortals call the Milky Way
> Speeds on, though imperceptible to eyes
> Alloyed of dust and moisture, to its goal
> Determined by Divine Intelligence.
> Your science can't encompass this, your eye
> Sees only twinklings faint, where galaxies
> Sweep on at cosmic speed. And all of them
> Consort together, intricately dance,
> Each its own destiny fulfilling straight,
> But interwoven with the others; all
> From the creation of the universe
> In splendid beauty hewing to God's will

     In testimony visible, a sign
     Of their Creator's majesty and might.

Most of the 'fat' in Krasicki's text lies in stanza two, the eight lines of which we have boiled down to two and a half: 'Your science can't encompass this, your eye / Sees only twinklings faint, where galaxies / Sweep on at cosmic speed'. I leave it to the reader's judgement whether here, and in other similar places where we have so streamlined the repetitive text, anything of value has been lost.

To return to my words at the outset of this section, in which I profess my devotion to respecting the original verse forms chosen by the poet, I recognise that, with my blank-verse rendition of the *Chocim War*, I stand open to charges of contradicting myself. I have no defence against the charge. In response, however, I would present the following thought that occurred to me on the same day I decided to abandon the Ariostan stanza for "Marlowe's mighty line." The Bavarian sculptor Ignaz Gunther (1725–1775) was a supremely talented artist. He was, however, born into a very unlucky century, as far as sculpture goes, for he came to age during the Rococo — that fainting, effeminate era so strongly in contrast with the virile splendour of the Baroque that precedes it, and the sober classicism of the Enlightenment, which follows. Whereas his light, dancing style is entirely appropriate for a work such as *Maria Immaculata* — a polychrome limewood carving which presents the Virgin almost as a contemporary damsel, complete with bled-white complexion and rouged cheeks — it simply does not work for a theme like *Christ at the Pillory*. That sculpture fails as a devotional object depicting one of the most savage episodes of Our Lord's Passion. Rather than engaging the onlooker's compassion and evoking tears, the overly-graceful, dancelike pose of the tortured Son of God makes it seem as if the sculptor were working from a snapshot taken at a discotheque. Some cultural periods, some artistic manners, are just not cut out for the expression of some subjects. The Rococo and high tragedy simply do not mix well.

And so, feeling that the epic wine of the *Chocim War* is best poured into the wineskins proofed by *Paradise Lost*, I abandoned Tasso. I acknowledge the fact that I may have contradicted myself in so doing, but I would rather think that I have created an exception, that proves my rule.

* * *

As always, I owe a special debt of gratitude to Ksenia Papazova and Glagoslav Publications for their continued support of Polish classics in English. I am also deeply indebted to the Book Institute of Poland for their financial support of this translation, and also the generous residency I enjoyed at their headquarters in Kraków, where the lion's share of this translation was produced.

Oczywiście, tę książkę poświęcam mojej kochanej Oli, która nie za bardzo myszy lubi, ale którą koty uwielbiają.

Kraków, 14 July 2019

THE MOUSEIAD

Canto I

Contents

King Popiel, degenerate son of better antecedents, having abandoned chivalric exercises, spends his life in feasting and delight. At first fond of mice, after coming into possession of the cat Mruczysław, he makes him his favourite, and decrees the extermination of mice throughout his realm.

> O you who sing of heroes' escapades,
> And make the world to stand agape in awe;
> If martial glory wins your accolades
> So that its fame you spread both near and far,
> Allow me too, my timid voice to raise,
> Though no Muse has inspired me a bard;
> A scribbler meek, I sing of no bold knights,
> But dip my humble quill to sing of gallant mice.
>
> 'Of gallant mice? What fame have rodents won?'
> Thus boldly cries the critic uninformed.
> 'The most inutile pests beneath the sun!
> Degenerate beasts, and justly held in scorn!'
> If so you think, just cast your eye upon
> Kruszwica's many grave-barrows forlorn!
> Those mounds the tales of bloody battles tell,
> When manly mice devoured the evil prince Popiel.
>
> There, broad and fertile fields border the lake,
> Gopło, of ancient and well-deserved fame.
> Its shores abound with lovely shade-trees, brakes
> Of ancient oak, birch, poplars' slender flames
> Wherein the feathered tribes their respite take,

Chattering the long day through at carefree games.
The valleys and green hillocks breathe and live,
Pleasing the human eye, with lovely perspectives.

Thus spreads the plain, until the eye is lost.
The farther on, the prettier, one feels —
The mead, with varied blossoms full embossed
Beneath its glorious border sways and reels,
While in the shade of each wisely-set copse
The herd, the flock, escapes the sun and kneels.
Cool in the thicket rest they, pair by pair,
The while their shepherd pipes his notes through the bright air.

There on the other shore, the city walls
Of Kruszwica — a splendid, well-built town —
Shine with their many buildings fair and tall,
Whose turrets soar storeys above the ground.
But the King's castle overtops them all,
Most wondrous, most deserving of renown,
Yet everywhere the eye should hap to light,
It will be dazzled, wonderstruck with great delight.

Here on the lake's smooth pane, Nature's delight,
An island seems to float — as ancient lore
Asserts, raised by a sorcerer's might,
And in its midst, a fortress grand doth soar,
With frightful towers challenging the height
Of heaven — like that Polish bird of war
That, carven there, the tribe of Krak declares
Here to reside, with Sarmatian Lech's glorious heir.

But Popiel, that degenerate son of brave
Forefathers, vainly boasts of their great deeds.
Slothful, of soft delight lethargic slave,
He delegates rule, lapped in luxuries.
All civic duty but befits a knave
He deems; the reins of state slip by degrees
From hands that royal excellence would measure

By base degrees of incomparable pleasure.
The favourites of this effeminate lord,
The harpies of the state, swollen with pride,
Insatiably suck his oppressed subjects' gore.
Their one aim: with the king to safe reside
Within these walls, and glut him with a store
Of empty bliss; so, cringing at his side
To serve themselves they prop his shaky throne;
Making him king in name — they make the realm their own.

Therein echoed no brave slogans of wars
Amidst the drunken gaiety of beasts;
Forgotten, all the battle-cries of Mars,
All manly pastimes had completely ceased;
There music tinkled, and there tittered whores,
While at their troughs men grunted at swinish feasts —
The copper gates were daily hung with roses
And in the sentry-boxes, nymphs struck comely poses.

Where once man's duty was set by God's law,
And so directed Polish mind and heart
That all the world beheld such men with awe,
Who raised prudence and courage to an art,
Degenerate Popiel, luxury's base thrall,
Infected all with shame, touched all with rot.
Forefathers' glories aren't worth a pin
When the land's poisoned with the reigning monarch's sin.

Virtue and vice expand from royal courts.
The simple folk who till field, and serve grange,
Learn their behaviour from the gentler sort.
Coltish in judgement, oft in action strange,
They watch how grand men do themselves comport,
From which their own carriage won't widely range.
Like herds of cattle, so the honest knaves —
Students of missteps, of passing fashion the slaves.

With his aberrant quirks, the base Popiel
Is ever shifting his deviant desires.
No person dare oppose the royal will;
By cringing, each to lofty grants aspires.
The king's it is, to keep one, or to kill —
And so his council fills with fawning choirs.
And so, on rages the orgiastic rout,
Only to pause, not with satiety, but bloat.

For nine days, he fancies a new caprice:
King Popiel is besotted with… the mouse.
The courtiers too, of course, fawn on the beasts,
Who gambol freely over field and house.
No fear they have of dirty feline deeds —
An open season on cats is announced,
And though the Tabbies put up a stiff fight,
No match are claws for the spear of a servile knight.

And yet, 'tis well the wiseman's words to weigh:
The wheel of Fortune is forever spinning.
Although she may well favour you today,
You mustn't think you'll be forever winning.
King Popiel was as feckless as was fey:
He loved mice, till a cat set his heart brimming.
So soon was he of rodent passion quit
As he met Mruczysław, his feline favourite.

Soon every flunkey's sweating out new ruses
To kill the mice, whose favour has elapsed.
This one is hard at work plaiting wee nooses,
That one's inventing snug and foolproof traps;
The craftsman's draughting complex subterfuges,
Like tiny guillotines; meanwhile, the cats,
Once more in favour, reprise their hunting grounds,
Where, long unculled, their wanted game thickly abounds.

The persecuted rodents now must tread
The paths of exile, forfeiting the homes

Where generations of mouse-tribes were bred,
The cosy nooks, where sires from pups had grown,
The cheese-filled larders, where they'd richly fed;
The kitchen, which they loved and called their own
No more with festive murine squeaking rings —
For mice are now outlawed to the badlands, poor things.

The famished eagle, driven from his aerie
Among the cliffs by hunger, with fell swoop
Will snatch a sparrow ambushed when unwary;
The startled squadrons, panicking, ungroup,
Each bird for himself, finding cover where he
May; trembling in fear, the whole scattered troop;
Thus were the mice dispersed, and run to ground,
The spectre of Cat looming behind the slightest sound.

Thus, wretched remnants wander the cold wastes;
Despairing dams seek pups without success,
Wee pinkies of their mothers find no trace,
And squeak out mournful wailings of distress.
The old campaigners, veterans of scrapes
With claw and springe, halt stock-still, motionless,
No matter what they're doing, where they're at:
Each rustle, each sudden shift of shadow, screams Cat!

Meanwhile the sad tidings spread far and wide.
Hundred-mouthed Rumour bruits to every ear
How now the cats wax mighty in their pride;
By king's decree, limitless and severe,
There is to be a rodent genocide!
And all the gnawing tribes shiver in fear —
Of varied nations, one nature they share:
No less than their small cousins, the rats, too, grow scared.

And who would not be moved, beneath such slings
And arrows as fall thickly on each hand?
At such a fatal feline threat, that springs
Straight at one's throat, at one's dear Fatherland?

Even the mind inured to caddish things
At such crises grows noble, brave, and grand;
The clever mind, struck, won't stay stunned for long —
What next transpired is... well, you'll learn in my next song.

Canto II

Contents

The persecuted mice and rats petition their king, Gryzomir, who reigns from Gniezno, to rescue his subjects from extermination. Thereupon follows a very tempestuous congress of mice and rats.

> The roads of happiness are slick and winding,
> Yet all the world barrels to the finish line.
> While these all virtue in the plebs are finding,
> Those others think the nobles half-divine.
> (These would among the faceless mob be hiding;
> Those pant in hopes of golden showers, in fine).
> Truth is, when Fate's inimical to your plans,
> Neither throne will prop you, nor will the average man.
>
> The reeling feet of Fortune widely range;
> She bows and pats our heads merely by chance.
> And though her verdicts skittish are, and strange,
> Still, ours is to fulfil what she commands.
> She needs mere moments kingdoms to derange,
> And errs oft in bestowing what she grants,
> Still all accord her latria divine,
> Though she be weak and crippled, and deaf, and blind.
>
> The squeaking nation, scattered at a blow,
> Determined to their king to make appeal —
> That Majesty enthroned was in Gniezno,
> The ancient seat of the murine commonweal,
> Safe on all sides from sudden rush of foe,
> Secure from feline stealth and mouser's creel.

King Gryzomir oppressed his subjects not:
Duly honoured by them; thereafter quick forgot.

On day appointed, they with tribute came —
Tokens of feudal troth, humble in nature:
Pork chops and lard, savouries of local fame,
They gladly gave a tithe of all they captured.
Heart-warmed by his vassals' love, he did the same:
Dispensing his largesse amongst his creatures.
'Twas not from want he welcomed these donations;
The royal larders full, he lacked not dainty rations.

Within a cloister grand his court was set;
A long, lax-tended, misruled monastery.
According to the founder's first intent,
The grand hall was to serve as library.
But following our age's gentler bent,
Transformed into meat-locker, larder, dairy,
The hall designed to nourish minds and souls
Now filled the monks' stomachs, and kept them round as bowls.

No greater lover of things folial
Than Father Canaparius, the unsung
Shredder of quartos, who papered the stalls
Of strictly catalogued ham, haunch and tongue,
Twisting his ginger fresh in cornets wrung
From octavo and codex! Old chronicles,
With all their pagan tales and impious trappings,
Far better served the cloister as greasy wrappings.

Thus grew the stacks of the old library
In volume, with the most delicate morsels,
Whence the discalced head of the priory
Pastured his humble, fat flock — the pour souls —
Thus bore they patiently Fate's vagaries
With low-slung bellies and humbly bent dorsals;
Thus, like the beasts that gathered at the crèche,
They humbly served their God, mortifying their flesh.

'Twas there, amidst the cheese and ham-filled stores
The mouse-king Gryzomir spent peaceful days.
Seeking no empty pomp nor vain honours,
Amongst these gifts of God he'd thriftily graze.
But when he heard the heartsick orators
With their sad omens of impending frays,
A council called he, and before the sun
Should set, he heralds bade with summonses to run.

Soon from all sides congregate the wise lords;
The grizzled oldsters, panting, crawling close,
While in rush the enthusiastic hordes
Of youth — each as if winged, swiftly goes —
So spurred they are by their wise ruler's words,
His to command, where'er he gauntlet throws.
So each one scurries, set to make his way
To stand to, be present, at the appointed day.

But first the noble ranks to entertain,
The king lays out a lavish royal feast.
And only when the councillors and their train
Are sated, from the greatest to the least,
Will he the solemn parliament convene.
And so that none refrain, but each one please
To speak his mind, he reads a binding oath
And opening address (the king himself wrote both).

It was like this. Since now each mouse had eaten
And every rat had thoroughly been sated,
The beadles saw each envoy meetly seaten,
Each Rat Deputised, each Mouse Delegated,
To speculate how to rally the beaten,
The nation from its peril extricatin.'
Above that squeaking caucus, one voice clearly
Sounds; it is the Speaker calling 'Hear ye, hear ye!'

The King then spoke, in tones of deep sorrow:
'Sad is the news, my subjects, that I bring.

Though I have kept you safe and hale till now,
Such are the threats which now about us ring;
So do our tribulations daily grow;
That you can hope for no aid from your king.
First in Kruszwica, now throughout the nation
We mice are faced with imminent extermination.

'So this is why I've called you here today:
That you might find some way out of this crisis.
I'm sure you sense what I don't need to say:
No time this, for broil 'twixt rats and mice is —
Your wits united must be put in play.
For should we fail — I shudder what the price is!
All rifts now heal, stifle all recrimination —
At least for now — toil together, for our nation!'

No vain words these, his call for unity;
For ages, both stirps of the rodent race,
Though kindred, would flare up in enmity
From time to time, injuring all estates
Unto the very loss of liberty.
Civil unrest undoes the proudest states!
Only non-rodent foes gain from such spats,
When rats quarrel with mice, and mice bicker with rats.

Chaos erupted when they were to vote
Upon the question which side first should speak.
The Rat-Maecenas strained with loud, full throat
To pierce the brisk cacophony of squeaks:
'Of precedence, there ought to be no doubt —
Ours is the right to veto and decree!
And if we suffer mites at this debate,
Let them heed, and submit, to what we legislate.'

A mouse, then: 'In what sort of court would he
Carry the day with such an argument?
Let's vote, and see who's in majority!
Because the rats are bulkier, brute strength

Is the foundation of authority?
In this arena, smarts, my honourable friend,
Must be triumphant, not gross might and main!
Let's spar with words, and see who has the bigger brain!'

The stour rages on with ferocity.
King Gryzomir's nearly knocked from his throne
As vainly he asserts his majesty,
While each one's true to his party alone.
The King cries: 'Rally, sons of liberty!'
In vain. Sweet Concord far away had flown.
He hears: 'Down with oppressive government!'
And thus dissolved the feuding murine parliament.

Canto III

Contents

Gryzomir, king of mice and rats, sends envoys to foreign lands in search of allies to aid in the struggle. At the same time he decrees a levée en masse. Mruczysław assembles the cats and prepares for war. At the first battle, the rats and mice are routed, and flee. But Filuś the cat, the favourite of Princess Duchna, is slain.

> Examples are strict taskmasters, in sooth:
> Both good and ill are fixed by precedent.
> What elders do, soon imitate the youth,
> And past *faux pas* remade in the present.
> Though no two things are quite the same, the truth
> Is that we schlep on well-trodden pavements,
> Chasing the fortune that we're sure we'll win,
> Threading the needle's eye, or the gaping gate of sin.
>
> For broad is vice's passage, virtue's, strait —
> And so, the surest route unto perdition
> Is in the multitudes to set one's faith,
> Hitching to errant guides our free volition.
> The rodents learnt this truth — alas, too late,
> When they fell out in intermicine friction.
> Fatal confusions checked each best-laid plan;
> This strife, I'm shamed to say, they learnt from the tribes
> of man.
>
> The council called their safety to secure
> Resulted in a greater peril still:
> As each one sought his prestige to ensure,
> Imposing on all others his own will,

Not reason reigned, but base *propre-amour*.
As concord waned, so waxed the nation's ill —
There, patriotism was the scarcest thing,
And few they were, true souls, who yet stood by their king.

'Twas they convinced King Gryzomir ordain
Envoys be sent to the surrounding lands,
The Polish rodents' danger to explain
And beg fraternal aid's chivalric hand.
To intervene, the neighbouring kings proved fain,
Which caused King Gryzomir's hopes to expand.
And so, enthused, without further delay,
The king decreed throughout the realm a general levée.

Meanwhile, as turmoil grows throughout the ranks,
The hag of strife from deepest Hell ascends;
Her stream of venom overflows its banks,
Blighting the shoots of war and government,
Hatred in hearts fostering a fungus rank,
The while the storm of revolt grows intense;
The fury cackles, flailing snaky locks;
The mice continue squeaking — the cats lick their chops.

For Mruczysław, the king of cats, with eyes
Indifferent could not behold the plans
Set now in motion by the martial mice;
Summoning the vassals that he had on hand,
Faithful retainers, these he in a trice
Sent forth to muster under his command
Each claw and fang that Katzendom affords —
And just in time! Behold: the mice advance in hordes.

O Muse! Who once, when vatic Homer nodded
O'er reams of dactylo-hexametric feet,
Roused him to deathless song murino-frogged,
If still you find poetic toiling sweet,
Come and inspire me that I might be lauded
As he was; deign that someday he might greet

Me as his compeer in such epic labours;
Nourish my thought; grant to me your bardic favours.
The left phalanx with foreign troops is miced,
Each rat resplendent, each mouse dazzling, all
Drawn up 'neath gonfalon and bright device.
The rodents from the Seine — fierce, beautiful,
Not only cats, but lions they despise!
They march to war as to a carnival:
Before the bugles sound the bold advance,
They toot their cornets, and with gay insouciance, dance.

The rats from the Danube, both tough and grim,
Like statues await the order to attack;
Those from the Tiber fear for their own skin,
But are adept at… sly thrusts to the back.
The Dniestrians' nature's hard as are their limbs;
No battle-glory do the Elbans lack;
The Cockney mouse can outdrink any cat,
So wild and savage he; the Swiss is true… and fat.

Less massive, but fearsome in quality,
The troops of Mruczysław feel their hearts swell
As he exhorts their knightly probity:
'The honour of all cats lies on the scale!'
Meanwhile, the massed rodent soldiery
Is fired by King Gryzomir's words as well.
From both sides then blares the call to advance,
And loud mewling and squeaking erupts on all hands.

The battling cats send forth such piercing screams
As never rent the amorous alley night;
The rats emit such angry chirps, it seems
As if all nature shrank before their might.
Mixed rat and cat blood rushes forth in streams,
While dust and flying fur obscure the light.
'Tis not with glaive and mace they duel; instead,
In vicious tooth and slashing claw, Nature is red.

Ruminogrobis, brave brother-in-law
Of Mruczysław, the fiercest of the fierce,
Led by example, flashing fang and claw,
And soon one mouse-captain, two colonels pierced,
He holds the battlefield entire in awe.
Him and his feral troops each rodent fears.
Though they may press him, and at times surround,
Soon are their corpses littered thickly on the ground.

And soon a rodent adjutant hastes near
Gryzosław, younger brother of the king
Of mice. No sooner did Gryzosław hear
Report of the wildcat-captain's daring,
Than secretly, and swiftly, from the rear
He falls on them with the entire right wing
Of mice, to set the cats in such a pother,
Rescue the pressed, and effect a fearsome slaughter.

There gallant Captain Miaukas bravely died;
Not far from him, fierce Dusimyszek fell.
No help to Filuś was the brindled hide
That lay upon the fop so snug and well;
Then all the cats fled like the ebbing tide,
When Myszogryz bade life his last farewell.
Th' exulting mice rush boldly to the kill
While the cat-ranks, their leaders slain, take to the hills.

Hearing his comrades' fear-redoubled cries,
Ruminogrobis, stunned, abstracted stood;
But when he saw them flee with terror-filled eyes,
An irate passion made to boil his blood.
Thirsting for new conquests, he thither flies
Against the current of the panicked flood.
With growing anger, rushes he to fight;
The more he eats, the greater grows his appetite.

The heap of slaughtered warriors higher grows
On both sides; then two adversaries rush

To meet each other — two implacable foes:
À bon chat bon rat — the latter champion much
Smaller, but the cat's peer in fame (so goes
Report); for the hunter, a worthy brush
To add to his trophies. All the field cede
To the two hetmans, biding the chivalric deed.

They pause; each measures each with savvy eye.
The cat notes that the rat is in fine fettle.
As is his wont, he lifts his prayers on high;
The rat, less pious, trusts to his own mettle,
And with impetus wild, see the rat fly
Straight at the cat's chest! When the dust settles,
The cat is stunned — did he give up the sprite?
The rat, well, as he bit, so on the rat doth bite.

The pain's so great, it makes the tabby reel.
He sweeps with claws — the rat skips to the side,
While in his maw bleeds half a feline heel.
Stumbling away, the cat sees the rat glide
For an oblique attack. Quickly he wheels:
The rat feels the cat's talons pierce his hide.
He struggles to break free — they roll on, tangled,
Till round his throat he's caught by the cat, squeezed, strangled.

Without their chief, the troops abandoned flee;
The feline force, though, have no strength to chase.
When from afar, the rout Gryzomir sees,
The wonted royal smile fades from his face.
For nought now: thundering, rebukes, decrees!
He begs the shirkers their steps to retrace:
And without looking back, soon sprints afar —
His subjects follow close their royal exemplar.

Nothing inspires as do a monarch's deeds!
The king in flight, all join the panicked trek;
Each legion back to its own country speeds,
Sensing a feline breath hot on their neck.

The native musters, and the foreign breeds,
All jump ship, like… well, rats at a shipwreck,
Their only comfort in their pell-mell flight
Is that evasion's aided by the shades of night.

Canto IV

Contents

The despair of Princess Duchna following the demise of Filuś: his funeral. Consumed with a passion for revenge, she begs her father to exterminate the entire race of mice.

O, that the flood of ages might retreat,
Restoring unto us the age of gold!
When 'neath Astrea's yoke, both light and sweet,
All creatures lived at peace, in one, kind, fold!
No legal traps lurked for unwary feet
Nor lust for gain rapacious hands made bold,
And that, which is the root of all our woe,
Slept hidden from all eyes, sunk in the earth, below.

Without that metal, nobody was poor,
Nor did red-clad patrician proudly strut.
After his toil, the farmer slept secure,
Snug in the comfort of his humble hut;
No judge misruled then from motive impure,
Nor usurer on other's sweat was glut;
No heir prayed death to gain inheritance,
Nor knight with hired murder did ever soil his hands.

Golden-haired Phoebus spreads his glorious rays
Refreshing, from on high, the night now through;
Nature dons a new splendour with the day;
Flower and herb revived shake off the dew.
The silent night is broken by the play
Of birds in the tree-tops that sing and coo,

But oh, Kruszwica's once delightful plain
Is now a spectacle of horror, death, and pain!

None but that hellish hag cackles with glee
As she surveys the carnage from on high
So many dead and merely maimed to see!
Her ears drink in so many a tortured cry!
Thus ends, poor fools, their yen for soldiery;
Glory fades as in agony they die.
See what a proud victory they have won:
The son mourns his father, and the father his son.

It's not long till Popiel's court comes to know
How many cats in battle met their doom.
The chaos and despair steadily grow
As anguished dames by turns wax wroth and swoon.
As fur in rage, now hair is torn in woe;
As blood in streams, now tears and sighs — monsoons!
The keeners' choir by Princess Duchna's led,
For Filuś, ah, sweet Filuś! Filuś the cat is dead!

Filuś delightful! Filuś kind and good!
Filuś who on each couch and bed would laze!
Filuś of graceful ballerino's foot!
Filuś who never fasted all his days!
Filuś abhorred of all the jealous brood
For how, and on whose breast, he snugly lay!
But now all that is past, the sun has set
On faithful Filuś; Duchna has no one to pet.

Eyes that were bright now of their light are spent;
She weeps, as does the court in sympathy.
Nought can console her — and so all lament
Poor Filuś, praising him most mournfully,
Including more than one tear-sodden gent
(Who sobs and weeps to mask authentic glee)
All wring their hands, dig furrows with their knees,
Preparing for the day of the cat's obsequies.

And so the ranks move off with mournful tread,
All with long faces, all eyes drowned in tears,
The troops of wildcats march at the very head,
With loftier brow, and with demeanour fierce;
Behind a standard of queer work are led
All the defunct Filuś's feline peers.
Funereal blooms enwreath the marchers' paws;
Retracted are all the sharp retractable claws.

Next come the friendly species, of each sort.
Each in their own way make their sorrows bare:
The birds voice warblings of mournful import,
The turtle-doves weep, pair after sobbing pair;
Even the impish squirrels dare not cavort,
As wailings multi-bestial fill the air.
Parrots are mute, to chattering once so fain;
Monkeys, decorously, from monkeyshines refrain.

Minette his collar bears, speckled pardine;
Hector carries a comb of ivory;
Iris a puff with gold embroidered fine;
Bebe flashes bracelets of prime category;
Milady a gold dish, from which he'd dine,
Sharing with friends a morsel, and a story.
Sad trinkets that on nape or paw he wore —
Ah! dear Filuś will have need of you... nevermore!

Upon a little golden bier is lain
The pet, deceased, of the forlorn princess,
Thick-strewn with blooms that fall like fragrant rain.
Beneath a shroud, rocked gently through the press,
His once so-cosseted earthly remains,
Now quite smoked-through with thick clouds of incense,
His crib-like coffin, thick festooned with crepes,
Is ported by the princess's best-beloved apes.

The august remains are now brought to the pyre.
Festooned in mourning weeds, draws near each knight,

Their emblems wreathed in black cypress boughs dire,
While Mruczysław intones the graveside rite.
Then all a reverent step or two retire,
And trembling paws set Filuś' pyre alight.
Both cat and pine-wood flame up in a flash,
And soon all that remains of brave Filuś is ash.

The remnants sad of a cat once so bold
Are deftly gathered by the reverent throng.
Filuś, exemplar of virtues untold,
Is praised in paeans of heroic song.
A jar is then brought forth of purest gold
Such as to regal interments belong,
In which his bones are lain; a sepulchre
Splendid receives them, on which lid is registered:

'Here Filuś lies, beloved of his Dame,
Who in his talents all his kind surpassed.
Pleasant to stroke, eager for every game,
The most faithful of companions; Alas!
Nothing remains now, but undying fame
And sad yearning regret, which shall not pass.
Gallant, but mortal, was the wound that he
Suffered on behalf of his nation's liberty.'

Weep at the glory shrunk beneath earth's lid:
The animal world's greatest ornament,
Ye lonely widows and ye tender kids,
All orphaned now at the cat's interment!
Too rashly did the Parcae snip the thread
Of Filuś' life! Too soon the veil was rent!
Now, each who passes near the cat's crypt sighs:
Alas! Here Filuś, sweetest tabby ever, lies!

Poor Duchna sobs, submerged in depthless woes,
But mourning, thoughts of sweet revenge won't quell.
The fair sex, timid? So the story goes!
But should some outrage make their anger swell,

Their hatred, like their love, no measure knows.
Those heavenly creatures flame as hot as Hell!
They shrink from no treason, baseness, nor shame,
That might help them to compass their determined aim.

Forgive my words, sweet nymphs! I've too much cheek.
Our duty 'tis your ev'ry whim to fulfil,
Attentive to command, your servants meek.
And yet the truth's a stricter mistress still.
Ungallant 'tis, of others' faults to speak,
But praise defects? That's indefensible!
Now, if unpleasant truths you must despise,
Shrug then and say: *The best poets tell the best lies.*

But back to Duchna. It did not suffice
That all the prisoners of war were slain
In vengeance, nor that all the banished mice
Trod now the sharp paths of exile in pain;
Uncomforted, with ever tearful eyes
She dinned her father's ears with the refrain:
'Relent not, Daddy! Bank the coals of hate!
Revenge Filuś! All the rodents — exterminate!'

The royal council urged him to decline
Her pleas; pettiness does not suit the throne.
Which way now should the royal will incline?
They counsel clemency; he'll make them groan!
Who has a soft heart, has a softer mind;
Where woman is, who calls his will his own?
Men rule the states that manly might erects;
Men rule the world… but men are ruled by the fair sex.

Canto V

Contents

Hard-pressed with hunger, Gryzomir enters a humble cottage and there falls into a trap. Upon returning home, the old witch who lives there first determines to kill him. But when she learns of his royal dignity, and his adventures, she grants him his life and sets him on her broom.

The fable often bears a moral sense;
Thus Aesop's laurel wreaths, undying, shine.
He does quite wrong, the fable who contemns —
Its flesh is sweet, though bitter be the rind.
Exquisite words the ear may well caress,
But if behind the song be no design,
Mere empty brilliance is but suavest form,
Which glows like rotting wood at night, but does not warm.

But now back to our tale. The battle lost,
Let's chase the mice who flee the battlefield,
By sore confusion and by terror tossed,
As they behold their scampering monarch yield.
He, though hard-pressed and by misfortune crossed
Has not abandoned quite his martial zeal;
Certain that he will wreak revenge one day,
For the time being, the valiant king… runs away.

O'er beaten path and trackless waste he hies,
And o'er his shoulder worried glances flings.
He turns back… pauses… and again he flies,
At every turning lurks the death of kings.
It's an old saw: *Fear has gigantic eyes.*
One might well add, *It has gigantic wings.*

Nimbler than hare that flees a hunter's nets,
Good King Gryzomir doesn't run, he fairly jets.

The while he thus in royal panic ran,
Upon the earth night did her mantle rest.
O, grateful hour for beast as well as man,
That soothes the labour-worn and the distressed!
Gryzomir sighed… then saw, quite near at hand,
A hut barely raised up from the earth's breast.
Hungry, he sniffed upon the breeze the spoor
Of… certainly a pantry… though lean-stocked and poor.

In his sore need of rest, the king creeps near.
He was in luck: half-open creaks the door.
Some dying embers chase the shadows drear,
Thrown from a peg where hang some rags well-worn.
The thin-thatched roof admits the atmosphere,
And when it rains outside, within it pours.
A spinning wheel, as if by wizardry
Turns (by wind-gusts moved) in short: naked poverty.

Upon a bad huswife our traveller's lit,
And yet the storm-tossed makes for any port;
Gryzomir's stomach's twisting him a fit —
He won't turn up his nose at any sort
Of nourishment; perhaps he was a bit
Incautious in his chasing every ort,
For as he filled his tummy, it so happed
He tripped a knavish spring, and in a flash, was trapped.

'O Fate insidious! O Fortune cruel and sly!'
Squeaks the poor mouse, imprisoned in the cage.
He calls for help; in vain. There's no reply.
He rushes at the bars, shakes them in rage,
To no avail. No matter how he try,
No effort might his sinking heart assuage.
At last, resigned, all hope away he flings
And sets to meditate upon the four last things.

Just so Bajazeth, that famed Turkish knight,
Who once made tremble all of Christendom,
The torch to set whole continents alight,
Though many crowns and sceptres he had won,
When checked in battle by a greater might,
Was shattered at the last, tripped up, undone,
And tasted Gryzomir's despair and shame,
A lonely slave, captive of the great Tamburlaine.

Soon did the rooster raise his raucous cry,
Announcing to the world the midnight hour.
The screech poor Gryzomir did terrify,
So shrill and near at hand the frightful stour,
It jostled him to set all worry by
(For one brief moment); once again to cower:
For just as soon as the cock's crowing died
Away, of a sudden the door burst open wide.

Then a strange creature, an old shrivelled hag
Came in, from journeying in foreign parts;
Her lips were livid; her pale cheeks did sag;
Her sunken eyes flashed with unholy sparks;
Only one tooth in her foul mouth did wag…
A witch! With all the identifying marks!
She'd barely wiped the sweat from her rank brow
When she caught sight of him: 'Well! What have we here, now!'

She grabbed the cage, slithering like a snake.
Gryzomir pressed back to the farther wall,
Making himself as small as he might make,
Curling himself into a little ball.
But then he rose, folded his hands, and spake:
'Madame, upon supplicant knee I fall.
Before you have me taste the bitter fruit
Of death, know that I am, of mice, king absolute.'

'I'm at your mercy, subject to your will:
Trapped fair and square, hoist by mine own design,

Yet — what glory would you win if you should kill
A helpless creature? The honourable mind
Recoils at such a thought — despicable!
Release me, and a greater treasure find
In upright action, and who knows? Some day
I might, though tiny, your benevolence repay.'

The old hag stood a moment still, disarmed.
How came he here? Her temper mollified
As at his tale she felt her cold heart warmed.
At last, her curiosity satisfied,
She let him go. The mouse-king, safe from harm,
Poured forth his thanks profusely. She replied
'Thus spins the wheel of Fortune, now in gloom,
And now in sunshine. Come, join me on my trusty broom.'

She spoke; at this, that faithful implement
Of its own will swept to its mistress' side.
Upon the handle Gryzomir was set,
Behind her. No sooner was she astride
The broom, lantern in hand, than they did jet
Quick up the flue, and soaring did they ride
The wind. The king of mice, his head aspin
With mortal fear, inched to the lamp, and crawled within.

There let him crouch beside the glowing tallow,
As through the clouds he swoops and skims and flies,
Piloted by the cackling hag unhallowed.
As they dare-devil it through the moonlit skies,
Their loops and barrel-rolls no more we'll follow,
But on Kruszwica once more train our eyes.
On flying mice we have digressed too long;
Of feline vicissitudes we must reprise the song.

Solemnised now was Filuś' funeral,
And Mruczysław, in battle, too, hard pressed,
Now felt the throbbings of his wounds in full
(For none too quickly had those wounds been dressed).

And he was old. The burdens of long rule
Will cause the halest royal cat distress;
He swooned. The court gasped with intaken breath,
For good King Mruczysław was duelling now with Death!

Soon swarming round him was Asclepius' tribe.
This one would cool him down, and that one heat;
This one a diet strict the king prescribes,
While that would stuff him full of fatty meat.
Fur flies at learned barb and diatribe;
'First, do no harm' was trod 'neath squabbling feet,
'Til Mruczysław bade each one 'Go to hell!'
Thus left alone to lick his wounds, the king got well.

Canto VI

Contents

The hungry rat, unable to resist the tallow, consumes the candle. Noticing that her light has gone out, the hag tosses the lantern away, and, with it, Gryzomir. Meanwhile, his brother Gryzander reassembles the scattered troops and leads them to the barn of a usurer.

Think not those raised aloft so fortunate,
Who soar the heavens with abundance blest,
Who from on high behold the lowly state
Of those adorers of magnificence
Who gaze at them… with something less than hate;
Who wish them ill, who laugh at their distress;
Such twists of fate would please them most of all:
For those who soar, plummet most steeply when they fall.

And so think not that this my bosom burns
With envy of high-flying mice and rats;
With lofty souls I shun familiar terms.
So as not to grow fat, I rather fast.
'Tis true, the witch did him a noble turn,
But how long will his soaring future last?
'Tis grand to fly, rocked on some cloudy berth,
Yet safer far, to tread the lowly, but firm, earth.

The night is dark; weakly the moonlight gleams
Behind the massive clouds, burly and thick;
Far below him, Gryzomir hears purling streams
As he speeds over wood, vale, cliff and rick,
The winds moan something frightful, and it seems
That our brave, half-dead knight… might just get sick.

He can see nothing, though encased in glass;
He'd like to scream for help, but would be too abashed.

Thus once did Astolf through the heavens zoom,
That bold and doughty knight of ancient lore;
Instead of straddling some vile witch's broom,
Upon the back of hippogryph he soared
In search of wisdom, past the gates of doom,
To where Orlando had his bed and board;
Now, he who would seek out where ours may lie,
Would fly in vain, it seems, however far he fly.

Thus Gryzomir his rash decision rued.
But what's to do now? All regret is vain.
And soon his guts clamoured again for food.
He smelt the tallow, on the candle trained
His hungry eyes… and saw that it was good.
At first from nibbling it he did refrain —
But then he sniffed again… he licked… he chewed…
Not long, alas! did he his stomach stuff;
For the candle, gnawed, toppled over, and was snuffed.

The witch let out a curse. Plunged into gloom,
Her navigation off, now flying blind,
She sought the reason for this misfortune;
What broke the lantern? Cause none could she find;
Nought knowing of the mouse king in the room
Of glass and tin, 'Who needs this now?' opined,
'Let it smash on those cliffs, for all I care!'
At this she launched the excess ballast through the air.

Below, Gryzander, he who led the rats,
Having a mile run, struck a heroic pose,
And of intrepid, manly nature, spat
Curses at heaven, bellowed frightful oaths;
Heedless of claws, squeaked dares at all the cats.
Hearing his voice, each rodent who cringed close

Took heart, for 'twas their hetman that did call;
And soon, round the rat-captain rallied one and all.

Gryzander, once, had gnawed Homer straight through.
(Some say 'twas ancient annals… all the same);
That ancient knights were eloquent, he knew,
And had digested orations far-famed.
And so the notion sparked in him and grew,
That now was time for him to do the same.
And so he scrambled up a nearby mound,
He coughed, wiped his nose, and thus began to expound:

'Brothers in woe, O my chivalric knights,
Through so much bloody fighting have we come
To this? Dirges, complaints, moaning and fright?
Why from the field of battle have you run?
Beaten and terrified — O, shameful sight!
Know this: through panicked flight no wars are won.
It's time to shake it off! Come, stand by me,
And claw of cat no longer fear, no farther flee!

'My brother may be dead, in prison pent,
Or maybe fleeter footed than are we.
Should we meet him again — which Heaven grant —
Let him behold our intrepidity!
Despair can be the bold's firm testament,
And more than once has led to victory.
Nothing can stain a rat but fear and shame.
Now is the time for rodents to win deathless fame!

'Hosts of reserves are rushing to our aid.
I have this news on good authority:
Caspian mice, rats from Meotian glade,
Squadrons allied from happy Araby;
And from the peaks Caucasian — whole brigades!
The savage Lydian and the Moor, thirsty
For blood; yet even should these not draw nigh:
Dulce et decorum est pro patria mori!

He'd barely done, when timid cries of joy
And murmurings of pleasure did resound;
As, at harsh winter's end, the sun deploys
His bright beams to unbind the frozen ground
And through the frigid air, warm breezes coy
Begin to breathe; the ice melts all around,
The herbs revive, the birds begin to sing,
And after winter sad, reborn is pleasant spring.

And thus the rodent hearts, filled with new zest,
Regrouped around Gryzander, whose advice
Was sought, after the rout, where they might rest
The harried legions of exhausted mice.
He gazed about the wilderness in quest
Of some safe haven, when there met his eyes
A barn, chock-full of grain from harvest gleaned;
'Thither!' he said, 'we march; to those fat magazines!'

A usurer, for forty years there breeds
Lucre and gallstones (with his flinty heart),
Having usurped the land with dodgy deeds,
Grown rich on toil in which he took no part.
Believing in no God, he worships greed
And raises stinginess into an art.
The heartless dastard, wasted thin with bile,
Is but the guardian of his unused, useless pile.

The land he filched each year would richly burst
With grain, no sooner ripe than strictly mown;
He rued the water with which he quenched his thirst
And blamed the sun because toll-free it shone.
Each year the unused grain heaps mildewed worse
While barn pests into massive throngs were grown;
There the mouse nation safely multiplies
Awaiting the promised advent of their allies.

But what of Duchna the unfortunate?
Up until now of her no one's inquired.

She weeps at Filuś's grave, cursing the Fate
That stole from her the pet she so admired.
To her despair she joins a savage hate;
Long mourning has her beauteous face bemired.
Each day, before the dawn expels the gloom,
You'll find her at Filuś's sepulchre, aswoon.

Popiel shed few tears at the cat's demise,
But his daughter's despair makes him care-worn.
Each day a fresh diversion he'll devise,
But what was rose once, now, to her is thorn.
Each suitor, who to her fair hand aspires,
However bright, is sent packing, forlorn.
For Princess Duchna never shall be wife;
To mourning, or revenge, she'll dedicate her life.

A king, to war with mice? Absurd! He shakes
His head; and yet her suriphobia's so fierce,
That when he thinks on her despair, he quakes.
Recalling what she lately vowed through tears,
He marshals a mouse-hunt, but, for Pete's sake,
The traps are empty! Nary a mouse nears
The cheese-spiked springe; and so he calls a feast,
To hear what his councillors might advise, at least.

Canto VII

Contents

Gryzomir's lantern falls to earth and lands upon the grave of Filuś. Taken prisoner, he is handed over to the princess, who sentences him to death. At the last moment, the witch rushes to Kruszwica, and rescues him.

> There is no sickness to be found on earth
> That does not have its healing antidote.
> Ah, you who would on men's minds prove the worth
> Of your prescriptions, think before you gloat:
> We've many moral maxims, but a dearth
> Of wisdom, such as true health might promote.
> Living is easy when all things are well;
> When Fortune fails us, wealth and reason go to hell.
>
> As long as Gryzomir was content to rest
> Where he was first set, clinging to the broom,
> He sat in safety. But, he had to test
> A better way — inside the cosy room
> Of lantern crawling; then, alas! he tempts
> His fate by nibbling, and trips his own doom.
> How true, that pride goeth before a fall!
> Wanting too much, we end up with nothing at all.
>
> The sudden vacuum took him by surprise.
> He knew not where he was, nor what to do;
> Jostled this way and that, Gryzomir flies,
> Pummelled and deafened by the gale that blew
> His fragile craft up, down, back, and sidewise,
> A plaything of the winds — the candle flew

Out the hinged pane, the papers all were shred —
Knightly Gryzomir holds on to the string, half-dead.

The stars began to fade then, as the sun
Shot forth the first rays of the coming morn,
And Duchna neared the grand mousoleum
Her much-bewailed Filuś again to mourn.
The cantor'd wiped his glasses and begun
Once more to sing the daily dirge forlorn
When, from the clouds, Gryzomir's lantern swooped,
Bonked him on the noggin, and knocked him hoop-the-loop.

'A miracle! Dear Filuś hears our song!
Call all the people!' Princess Duchna cries —
Startled she was, at first — but not for long —
She takes this for a sign: *Woe to the mice!*
The cantor (rubbing his nut where 'twas bonged)
Grins with content, as Gryzomir he spies
Unconscious in the wreckage, but alive;
He snatches him, and bears him to Duchna captived.

No miser's eye at gold ever so sparked,
No tippler's at the brim-full pot of sack,
No conman's, chancing on an easy mark,
No doctor's, meeting hypochondriac,
No hypocrite's, who sees a rival stark
Bereft of virtues that she herself lacks
Than Princess Duchna's, at that fateful hour
To see the King of mice, helpless, and in her power.

Meanwhile the hag (haltingly, by degrees
For lack of headlamp) started her descent
To the enchanted mount, battered by trees
She'd knocked against, but now dark night was spent.
The birds began their matin harmonies,
The beasts awoke, snuffling the new dawn's scent,
When, bruised and battered, whirled by headwinds round,
At last, on Bald Mountain, she safely touches down.

She glances back, and to her horror sees
The seat behind her's empty! The rat! Where?!
Like wounded lioness she roars; she's seized
With guilt and pain — too reckless through the air
She soared and rolled! Plunged deep in miseries
She beats her pate (she had no locks to tear),
Groans in contrition, wails; to tell the truth,
Had it a partner, from grief she'd've ground her tooth.

To sorceries and well-wrought spells of yore
The witch then set herself — no time to lose —
She draws a circle on the ground with lore
In ancient letters circumscribed, then throws
Handfuls of charmed herbs, magic dust, and more,
Squalling the while beneath her crinkly nose.
Before she'd finished with her mystic rhymes,
She'd whirled herself dizzy, like a dervish, nine times.

The air is filled with her blood-curdling cries
As she summons the potentates of Hell,
(On every nearby nape the hackles rise),
From deep within the earth a rumble swells
And Lucifer from his black throne near hies,
And with him flocks of spirits damned, as well.
The stars no longer let fall their sweet rays
And, veiled in bloody gore, the moon now hides her face.

Blindworms and reptiles gibber in delight;
Vipers crawl forth when she but nods her head;
The earth quakes, riven with blue bolts of light
And Nature, stunned, seems about to drop dead.
The storm grows worse, the gale winds wax in might
And ancient oak roots tear from out their beds.
She gazed about and saw that all was good,
Then set to cast some bolder spells... because she could.

The devils, at her omnipotent command
Revealed to her how Gryzomir was vexed.

A captive, gripped in Duchna's angry hand,
How he came there… and what would happen next.
Secrets? From women? Keep them if you can!
Content at the results of her strong hex,
Needing no lantern now that it was dawn,
She hopped her broom, and soon, Kruszwica-ward was gone.

The court spent little time in vain debate.
Guilty they found Gryzomir of his crimes
Both old and new. Soon off to meet his fate
Was he marched under guard, and made to climb
A scaffold, upon which a pyre sate:
High, visible, with oil and kindling primed.
The cantor, whining still of his bruised brain
Was given the honour of setting pyre aflame.

The witch then groaned with pity, seeing these
Dire preparations; how to free her knight?
Could she but vengeance plot? Then, by degrees,
An inkling grew… Could it work? It just might…
She sprinkles powder: "Choo!' the people sneeze.
The cantor sneezes… noses tickle, bite…
The whole crowd's blind with sneezing, king and court,
(For what kings do, their minions mimic, *comme il faut*).

Taking advantage of the hangman's sneeze
(Indeed, of universal sternutation)
Gryzomir slips from out his fetters, flees,
And as all *'Chooed*! and *'Chooed*! in consternation,
Escaped. He hadn't gone far, when he sees
The witch, who'd saved him from the conflagration.
While the whole nation sneezed and hacked and coughed,
Her sides were fit to burst, so jollily she laughed.

As soon as she the sprung mouse-king espies,
She calls him to bestride her trusty steed,
Wiping the tears of laughter from her eyes.
No sooner clomb he on, but with all speed

The broom, the witch, the mouse soared in the skies.
To coax him on, this time there was no need:
He'd learned his lesson: better far to fly
Than plummet; once bit (as the saying goes) twice shy.

Alas, had he but kept open one eye
I'd have been grateful to his majesty!
How splendid must the view be from on high:
Meandering river and proud city,
The pearls of architecture to descry...
The heart would soar at the mere memory!
Had he not kept his peepers clamped in fright,
What profit to poet! To reader, what delight!

Meanwhile, below, the scattered army's led
In Gryzander's fat silos to regroup;
After their tiring march, he has them fed
And rested, while he ponders his next coup.
What he's unsure of will remain unsaid —
Where might Gryzomir be? And so, the troop
Gets a nice furlough. To renew the wars
He's in no hurry. First, he must augment his force.

Eftsoon his faithful spies brought the report
From Kruszwica of Gryzomir's dire plight:
How he'd been in a pickle, how the court
Was stricken with The Sneeze which fostered flight,
And what a flight it was! Indeed, he soared!
And this one fact befouls his true delight:
His brother, absent from his fellow rats,
Has put on haughty airs? And flies about with bats?

Canto VIII

Contents

At the advice of his counsellors, King Popiel declares a war on mice. Gryzomir, meanwhile, is transported by the hag to the banks of the Rhine, where Serowind, leader of the rats there, who had recently devoured the Elector of Mainz, promises his aid. That promise given, Gryzomir returns home.

It's an old saying, but none the less true:
'There are as many opinions as heads.'
People like nothing better than to argue —
(If you need it to be more simply said).
'Tis a misfortune rightly to be rued,
Which no one ever remedies; instead,
Let four or five but gather in a room:
No problem will be solved until the Day of Doom.

Popiel a council called, of hand picked peers,
The matter of the mice to contemplate.
The first one jumps: 'Ahem!' his throat he clears,
And in terms florid starts to perorate
'On these so many, glorious, golden years
Through which our King has steered the ship of state…'
And on he blathers, with so many sage, wise
Platitudes, no one can get a word in edge-wise.

'What boots Garamantene ferocities,
Or the knights, wide-famed, of Maeotic lands?
Those fateful Bythinian victories,
Or the hardy bucklers of Ceylonese bands?
King Popiel's greatness towers over these

To thunderous ovations of uncounted hands
That raise their thanks sincere to Providence
That so splendiferous a monarch to this nation grants.

'Your have, Your Majesty, far surpassed all
Your glorious antecedents, and have raised
Your realm to heights Atlantean. Weak and small
The titans in comparison! Of days
Begone and future — you, pontifical
And vatic link — but let me pause my praise:
Your Majesty, take voice, your nation pleads;
Your wisdom perspicacious, this subject people heeds.'

He paused to catch breath. The Prime Minister rose
(Spying his chance); coughed in his fist, once, twice,
Removed his spectacles from his arched nose,
Assumed a pose rhetorical, blinked his eyes,
And loudly declared: 'Well merit those
Rodents severe punishment! May this apprise
All subjects of King Popiel near and far —
Rebel or recusant, all shall quail before the law.'

Then the Chancellor of the Exchequer
Took voice: 'You know what the mice have been doing?
Bleeding the purse, the little beggars!
They're nibbling, gnawing, causing ruin
To barn and silo, the nasty wretches!
We've been too *laissez-faire*, it's true, and
Unchecked, their numbers wax larger each day,
Growing fat by theft while we sleep — now they must pay!'

And round and round whirl unending debates
(In every council chamber it's the same):
Sub-Treasurer Prime Minister berates,
Prime Minister quite squarely sets the blame
At the Field Marshal's feet, while he, irate,
Lambastes his hetmans: 'Get on with the game!
It's war!' Even back benchers yelp and snap

(To prove they do more in parliament than just nap.)
Then when it's time to separate in blocs
And count the votes — Come on, are you surprised?
Quite evenly the lobbies fill with frocks
— There are as many *Noes* as there are *Ayes* —
For each and every member but takes stock
Of his perspective — only he is wise;
Unable to enact a single bill
On mice, they tell the king: 'My Lord, do what you will.'

Only one of the older senators
Took no part in the vote; long shunned, disgraced
For his devotion to the nation's laws
And other trifles, who neither wore lace
Nor fancied cats and lapdogs, verses, balls…
— How dare he show his raw unpowdered face
To bore us with amendments and the rest
Of that legislative claptrap? And so drably dressed? —!

At last, it was decided that no more
The matter should be just left to the cats.
A solemn declaration of war
Was ratified, and quickly drawn up pacts
'Twixt man and feline were readied for paw-
print and signature; spears were slipped from racks,
Bucklers and bombs made ready by the dozen,
Which made Mruczysław grin… like his Cheshire cousin.

Now, while he readies his four-legged army
For the allied assault, it's time to check
On Gryzomir, who, set on the broom calmly
Now, gave the hag free rein, neither cares nor recks
Where she will take him; so grateful, he warmly
Thanks her and thanks her for saving his neck…
So what if she's addicted so to flight?
What can he do? but grit his teeth, and hold on tight.

Although his eyes are shut, he feels and hears
The wind as the broom whizzes through the skies.
Then, suddenly, his stomach rushes near
His throat as the broom pitches, and declines
Terra firma-ward. Then there meet his ears
Of mice unnumbered squeals and squeaks and cries —
The broom skims, touches down, and before long
Gryzomir is surrounded by an awestruck throng.

It was a festive rodent convocation
Of all the rats from both sides of the Rhine.
Festooned with laurels, 'twas a celebration
Of the grand, crushing triumph of the time:
The Mainz Elector's fierce annihilation
By vengeful — and hungry — legions murine.
No tower, nor island refuge was worth a rap:
The storming rats ate him up, leaving not a scrap.

This really happened. Wonders often do.
What's handed down should not be cast in doubt;
It's written — see? In print. It must be true.
From frequent repetition, the truth will out!
Rats oft prevail. I believe it. Don't you?
Why — even today. Just have a look about!
Let's nod in public (in private, we may smirk).
But now, enough digressions. Let's get back to work.

Soon the rejoicing turned to shocked distress
As Gryzomir's sad story met their ears.
The Rhineland rats grew more and more perplexed,
And joy triumphant soon gave way to tears.
The masses stood in silence, as if hexed,
When the old witch stepped boldly forward. Near
The King she took her place, and when she spoke,
Such words addressed she to the awestruck rodent-folk:

'Majestic Lord, and you, O knightly rats,
Whose valorous deeds amaze the world entire,

I here request of you a martial pact
In this most anxious hour, bloody and dire.
If you be warriors, now's the time to act!
Your battle-tested powers are required.
Though you be small, you're tough in heart and thew —
It's time to show the world again what you can do!

'In solidarity with him I stand,
Your brother rat, whom you see to my right:
He, King of rats and mice was, in Poland,
Where he ruled in abundance and delight;
But Fortune then dealt him an adverse hand,
And, to save life and limb, he took to flight.
Tested by fate inimical, severe,
He thus makes bold to supplicate you, his brethren, here!'

Then she began the story to unfold
At greater length, concerning the late broils:
How the antipathy at first took hold
And how — at the start — it might have been foiled;
How both the warring sides took their first bold
Offensive steps toward the bloody moil
Of war; who joined, and who deserted, ranks,
And who, for the catastrophe, most deserved the thanks.

But when she warmed up, and in fine detail
Began expansively to sing of each knight's
Bold deeds; of peace overtures doomed to fail;
Of paw-to-paw combat; of the fiercest fights
'Twixt cat and rat, whole hours away did sail…
And still she droned, as morning turned to night.
So ardent, and exhaustive, was her story
That soon both audience, and hero, were snoring.

The old hag spoke so long, at last she yawned
Herself. She paused, she sighed, she looked around…
And what did her dismayed eyes light upon
But all the rats stretched out upon the ground!

All snoring peacefully, from king to pawn!
Insulted, angry, she howled like hell-hound
For her e'er-trusty broom… Which did not leap
To its mistress' side — for it too was fast asleep.

She grabbed it by the neck and raised it high
In ire above the snoring rodent heads.
King Serowind awoke in time and spied
The looming danger; abjectly, he sped
To beg her pardon, swallowing his pride,
Placing the blame on revelling, instead
Of her… eloquent epic; mollified,
She was won over with gifts rare and dear,
And Serowind pledged assistance to Gryzomir.

Content at having thus compassed her end,
And by his gentle flattery quite soothed,
The witch prepared her homeward way to wend
While Gryzomir (still groggy, to tell the truth)
Sought out some means to slip his flying friend,
While at her winged steed he glared in ruth.
So, bidding a silent farewell, he hops to it,
Sneaks out of her sight, and heads for home, safe, on foot.

Canto IX

Contents

Gryzomir again leads the troops. Popiel is in despair, as the battle of mice and cats ends with the death of Mruczysław, who falls in a peculiar duel at the hands of the same Gryzomir, king of rats.

When I was a young man, I too would set
Out on a trek — no different from the rest.
Most often, such vain ramblings I'd regret,
Returning home bedraggled from the quest,
Having accumulated nothing… but debt.
Pilgrims who profit? Few they are, and blest!
For most who travel long, pain is their guerdon;
Pain self-inflicted, and to their hosts, a burden.

Too lightly did he the decision take,
Our knight, to hoof it to his fatherland
When he his trusty pilot did forsake;
He parted, too, from King Serowind's band
Of rats victorious, but first, the latter spake
Such words of promise: 'Here you have my hand
(Or paw, rather), pledging our fealty;
No longer fear; what Rhineland rats can do — you'll see.'

There, where through fertile field and pleasant park
The Rhine meanders, ravishing the eye,
At that time, the Hercynian Forest, dark
And thick with brush stood, filled with cry
Of hungry she-bear echoing off the bark
Of ancient oaks… Fancy a stroll? Not I!

But Gryzomir, bold with patriotic love,
Gave not a fig for hungry bears, come they in droves!

He suffered much; such burdens did he bear,
Where is the vatic pen that might express
The tight escapes of rodent hide and hair
Of doughty Gryzomir, so oft oppressed
By mortal enemies? On land, by air,
With wit and elbow-grease on our hero pressed;
No luxury could tempt his honest heart
From fighting on, here with might and main, and there
                                                  with art.

O sacred love of fatherland! Indeed,
Only by honest, pure minds art thou known.
For thee, poison tastes like the sweetest mead;
For thee, no heavy fetters weigh one down.
'Tis thy power heals the crippled limb, and feeds
The mind with happy nourishment alone!
'Tis glory in thy noble cause to fight;
To live in want is joy, to die for thee — delight!

Not distant now, the Sarmatian frontiers!
The closer he, the more his mind is thronged
With thoughts of joy and pain, with hopes and fears.
Soon shall he see the land for which he's longed,
And though the path's made rough with toils and tears,
Although he's tired and footsore, he keeps strong
Recalling that he'll soon rejoin his kin —
At this thought, Gryzomir catches a second wind.

And soon he's there — where through wide-spreading lands
The rapid Warta foams its riversides;
Thinking to group again his scattered bands,
He oft descends the highroad for the byes;
Recalling those snatched by Bellona's hands
Tears of remorse and pity fill his eyes;
Thoughts of revenge chase from his mind all peace;

He hates war, but till it's won, from warring he'll not cease.
Into the Warta then Gryzomir leaps,
Despite the stormy heavens, the steep banks,
Stunned both by cold and current, he braves the deep,
And now he's tossed on high, and now he drank
A lungful, sunk — still his devotion keeps
Him striving, till, tired, proud, and full of thanks,
He scrambles onto the beloved strand
After so many labours, by air, water, and land.

Soon did the miser's barn loom into sight,
And round it, hordes of mice and rats. He neared
The barnyard, judging that the time was right
Before his loyal subjects to appear.
Soon there erupted shouts of pure delight
In honour of kind, clement Gryzomir
(Who amnestied the shirkers); ratified
Anew as King, he smiles, and all rush to his side.

Now, none of the Sarmatian levies stirred
With such martial zeal at Popiel's command.
The war was so undignified, absurd!
They'd be the laughingstocks of every land!
And so Popiel went back upon his word
And to his island fastness swiftly ran
Ne'er to peep out again. Mruczysław, irked,
Still rolled his sleeves up (so to speak) and set to work.

While the cat-king prepared for the onslaught,
Popiel 'Lelum Polelum!' solicits in tears;
Adverse, alas! the oracles are brought,
And like Heaven's scourge the murine army nears.
Soon the first bloody skirmish will be fought,
As (tiny) drums and bugles meet one's ears;
Exhorting all, Mruczysław firms his lines,
While Popiel scampers into his cellar, and whines.

Serowind led the phalanx on the right,
Heading the corps of Rhenish river-rats.
Gryzander, who'd once been Popiel's delight,
Who feared nor fang nor claw of any cat,
A worthy pattern of mouseliest knight,
So fierce of mien, ferocious in combat,
Commanded the left wing of cavaliers;
The midmost warriors, of course, were Gryzomir's.

Now was no time for ardent martial speech —
Both armies, flaming with hatred and ire,
At once fell fiercely grappling, each to each;
Fear had no room in hearts that were afire
With desperation; howl and mewl and screech
Soon filled the skies, the earth trembled entire,
While clouds of dust toward the heavens soared.
Blood flowed in rivers; the plain was mired thick with gore.

Two blazing torches — just so seemed the eyes
That flashed beneath the brow of Mruczysław —
So horridly the rats they terrorise.
Gryzomir too, of stout heart, iron claw,
Martial example to his troops supplies:
Smashing the feline fang, taunting cat's paw,
He gnaws, he slashes, charges, feints and swoops —
Then spies Mruczysław menacing the Rhenish troops.

Old Serowind, despite his many years,
Of ancient valour, fighting-fettle sound,
Above the fray his massive frame he rears,
Nor to his enemies gives any ground,
Supported on all sides by brigades fierce
Of sons and grandsons that encase him round;
Swelling with warlike will and bravery,
They hurl themselves upon the cats, who panicked, flee.

Alarmed by his routed fellows' cries,
Mruczysław races there, whence others flee.

Beneath his claws soon Gomułkiewicz lies,
The famous chief of the Third Century;
Szperkas, next to brave Twarogus, then dies,
His orphaned children never more to see.
No ruse availed that many-wiled mouse
Serosław, who perished, and with him, all his house.

Parmesanidas then, from the left side
(Serowind's much-loved son, beautiful, brave),
Seeing the Rhenish king so sorely tried
Raced up, in hopes his dear father to save.
Alas! noble Parmesanidas died —
Crushed in the jaws of his cruel enemy.
Serowind looked on with despairing eye;
His son dead, he wished for nought now, save to die.

Then suddenly, 'twas Gryzomir that stood
Before Mruczysław; now the time had come
To bring a final end to their long feud.
A combat was determined, one on one.
Abstracted stood the armies, for what could
They do but in amazement pause, look on
And pray: To whom would fall the victory?
Before they fought, the rat-king addressed his enemy:

'Be not so bold, you braggart! Set apart
Your puffing and your preening. For your frame,
As large as it may be, cows not my larger heart.
Pride goes before a fall; petty the fame
I'll win by laying low such an upstart!
Mewl on and hiss! To me it's all the same;
And when you lie, rigid in mortal pallor,
You'll prove how vain boasts shrink before mousely valour.'

This having said, he raised his glance on high,
And there beheld… the witch astride her broom!
His heart swelled more at the auspicious sign
Which augured for the feline legions doom.

Yet Mruczysław the bold, unmortified,
Was sure the rat would shortly ford the gloom
Of Hades at his… paws, but did not say
A thing, for both combatants rushed now to the fray.

What wondrous deeds of arms were then displayed
By two brave knights of the first quality!
With streams of blood chivalric blushed the clay,
But not a jot ebbed their harsh enmity —
Both awe-struck armies looked on, mouths agape
To witness what haps when ferocity
Is spurred by heroism; mighty, majestic
Mruczysław was, Gryzomir brave, adept, and quick.

Three times they rushed to grapple, the fierce pair;
Three times their thick blows thundered all in vain:
Cat tears at rat, rat cat, and through the air
Fur flies; they battle foe and their own pain,
Their strength augmented by faith, and despair,
Each blow is torture, but on they strike again.
The awestruck Parcae paused passing their thread
As for the fourth time, the panting foes together sped,

But only briefly. Implacable Fate,
Which rules all creatures, balanced on its scales
The destinies of both. Inviolate,
Unbiassed its decrees; the rat's dish sails
Aloft; the cat's sinks down. For him awaits
His final mortal act; his strength now fails,
As does his boldness; Mruczysław the cat
Falls broken at Gryzomir's feet — and that… is that.

Canto X

Contents

Learning of the cats' defeat, Popiel drowns his despair in drink. Then, as the mice and rats begin to draw near, he takes a boat to the lake island, but the rodents catch him up all the same, fall upon him, and devour him.

Were I a king, or suchlike lofty wight,
I'd try to rule my subjects by the heart.
The people's love assures the monarch's might,
From it, all other blessings take their start.
What boots a loyalty enforced by fright?
To win their gratitude would be my art.
Mere wealth and arms are petty things. Above
All royal treasures is a loyal subject's love.

Yet subjects well-disposed are rare indeed;
No one enjoys being ordered about.
The honest servant, too, 's a dying breed:
Uneven ranks leave a bad taste in the mouth.
Resent comes from impetuosity
In judgement — raising up and casting out
On pretext slight, conniving… in a word,
Who's to blame if servants grumble? Who else? Their lord.

Such troubles plague even the good and wise.
What then of Popiel, king and epicure?
'Twas he began the war, 'tis he that flies
As soon as, to his horror, he'd made sure
Of the approaching hosts of vengeful mice.
He can't bear to look on battle, though immured

Within thick walls; he flees, he tires, at last,
He stopped and drank his full of mead, and out he passed.

Sunk deep in sleep, in dreams before his eyes
His poisoned forefathers, in sad parade
— The nation's glory once — gloomily rise,
In mourning now, who once had been arrayed
In victors' laurels. Popiel, in such wise
Pierced with remorse, and with terror half flayed
That barely he could rule his respiration,
Must now give ear to their dark denunciation.

'Of sire emasculated, worthy scion!
In villainy and sin so foully sunk;
Who wages war on mead alone, and wine;
Of the whole kingdom the preeminent drunk —
Ne'er shalt thou learn thy nature to refine,
Ever to wallow in base, sodden funk!
See what thy luxuries do now bequeath!
Thou vile creature — deserving but the vilest death!'

Before his eyes they set a looking-glass.
He gazes… and therein what wonders spies!
In a long line, his heirs and issue pass,
So lifelike, he averts his panicked eyes.
From his mead-cups emerges the first Piast,
Then his bold, greedy son does next arise,
And on, and on — these brave, of waxing might;
Those others feeble, waning, mired in base delight.

By drink undone, so many a great soul!
By vodka Lech and Mieszko were tripped up,
Like Bolesław, for valour called the Bold,
Who drowned his virtue in Kievan cups,
And splendid Przemysław, who was brought low
By drinking much too deeply while he supped
On Mardi Gras; even Great Casimir
Tippled with Esther in Łobzów, or so I hear.

Olbracht, in Kraków, with an axe was brained
When, drunk, about the Market Square he prowled;
And Stefan — that Stefan! of martial fame!
Drank death in Grodno, at some tavern foul;
Władysław, so worthy of our acclaim,
At last podagra made to sit and scowl;
Odd royal deeds come of inebriation —
Saxon August made a sponge of the whole nation!

Tormented, half dead, Popiel's roused from sleep
By a commotion, growing, overhead.
Rushing in panic through the castle keep,
He calls and calls — all's silent — all have fled
Before the rodent hosts that closer creep.
He'd like to parlay — but what might be said?
Shaken, abandoned, parasites all flown,
Abjuring their oaths, leaving him wretched, alone…

Swiping some petty cash, the PM ran
(Swiping the seal too, 'Let's see what comes next');
No battlements forgetful marshals man;
The senate declares *depositus rex*,
Cursing the late king's rule and all his clan.
The mead all drunk, the grooms took to their legs.
The honest chancellor fled the Treasury:
Absconding with the strongbox, he left behind the key.

The tonsured cantor, who intoned the hymns
In praise of king and cat (when all was well)
Seeing the castle ranks begin to thin,
Sensing the king's last hour was soon to knell,
— Always the poet! — as he once had been
The king's windbag, now felt the spirit swell
Inside him with a paean to the Rat,
Never again (for now) to sing in praise of Cat.

Abandoned thus by all the servile folk,
Seeing the angry rats like dog stars near,

No cry could squeeze through his petrified throat,
But even should he call, pray, who would hear?
Then he espied, on the lakeshore, a boat,
And in it, the senator, whom he would fleer,
Whom, as he never flattered, grovelled, prated,
The courtiers all despised, and King Popiel hated.

He broke down sobbing, the late-remorseful king,
And all the more, when he beheld prostrate
The man before him: 'O, fortune's playthings
We all are, but too sore tested by Fate
Are you, Your Majesty. Come, let me bring
You somewhere safe. Your foes are near, and great,
But I'll transport you to some safer ground,
Or by your side I'll share your lot; we'll both go down.'

They hop into the skiff, but then the winds
Fall on them suddenly from every side,
Bearing them straight to where, with Serowind
In front, the rodents breast the rolling tide.
Now did the monarch's final act begin.
Fiercely the senator his paddle plied,
But then the king into the flood did fall
Where the rats ate him up: hair, and hide, and all.

O great Kadłubek! Yours the laurel bough —
You first sang of King Popiel, and sang best,
And for this fruit sprung of your sweaty brow,
For age upon age be you richly blest!
Forgive my muse, too jocund, but allow:
Wisdom is best imparted, with a jest.
And whether chronicle or fairy story
You wrote, your meant well; to you, undying glory!

Now we, who've listened to this epic tale,
To the good man, the author, let us raise
Our thanks that he the story did retail.
Who drink its flood, bedeck the spring in bays.

Sneer at the humble not, ye great ones; rail
Not against the great, ye humble, but praise
Him who teaches sweetly. Readers, Friends,
Be gracious, be indulgent... here my labour ends.

END OF THE MOUSEIAD

MONACHOMACHIA
OR
THE WAR
OF THE MONKS

Canto I

Contents

Discord, jealous of monastical peace and quiet, enkindles the flames of rebellion amongst the sons of Dominic. Assembled in council to decide how to meet a threat posed by their envious rivals, the Dominican fathers determine to summon the Carmelites to a disputation.

Not all is gold, what glitters, that's for sure.
Nor is he bold who roundest puffs his chest.
'Tis not appearance that determines nature;
One's heart gives courage, not the way one's dressed.
Hoods no less than helms fierce blows endure,
And monks, no less than knights, stand to the test.
Cloisters are no refuge from envy's sting —
And of just such a war I now propose to sing.

I sing of civil war, and here declare
It shall be cruel, though lacking swords and darts.
The knights shall be discalced — and almost bare;
Protected only by the manly parts
They play; a war of monks. Don't laugh! Be fair:
Show me the son of Adam free of warts!
Laugh if you must, then. But though you may rail,
Of the martial deeds of monks shall be my tale.

Once, in a city, the name of which I'll keep
In pectore (in sum, what's it to you?),
'City' defined as some scattered brick heaps,
Worthy retreat of peasant and of Jew;
City (I say, and legally enfeoffed!
A lord lived near, in a crumbling castle, too);

A damn foul city! Here, three taverns, there:
An arch in ruins, cloisters nine, hovels to spare.

In this so-called provincial capital
A reverend dullness had its ancient seat.
Sheltered beneath an august temple's wall,
Whose inmates orthodox could pray, and eat.
The faithful folk were at the beck and call
Of cloister bell (the monks' renown was great)…
Divine simplicity! Who'll hymn a song
Worthy of thee…? Eh, some other time. Let's move on.

Of Saturn's reign we've fables by the score,
Penned mostly in the Gold or Silver age…
Happy the Prior, who eats enough for four!
Happy the Lector at his mystic page!
Happy the Father, who unruffled snores
However Nocturne or Matins might rage!
Happy the Brother, who, the night-lamp doused,
Tumbles with dry-rung wineskin upon his cot, well-soused.

Just such, in short, was the delightful lot
Of our holy do-nothings. Ah, but cruel Fate,
Who human peace and gladness values not,
Whom turns of ill-fortune seem to elate;
Who happy sunlit scenes delights to blot,
On weakest backs imposing fardels great,
Who topples thrones and nations… O, most foul!
Wilt thou now stretch thy spiteful hands toward the cowl?

Long ages had elapsed since those wars dire,
Which once filled all the world with awe and fright;
In calm contentment dwelt the Seraphic friar,
And no one thought to cross the Carmelite;
The Preachers' Order trained no words of fire
Upon capriote or habit brown or white;
Long since the stormwinds of dissension ceased,
Even the Hospitallers lived in blessed peace.

But then that hag, who through this vale of tears
Flits often — Discord — on our woe to browse,
The same one, who in Homer, Paris steers
From safe Mount Ida to that fatal house
Where Helen dwelt — beholding the monks' good cheer,
Determined in her ire the same to douse.
So, swooping low, she cast down through the air
A knot of vipers that she'd just plucked from her hair.

She shook her torch, and sparks of sulphur flew
Down upon cloister roof and tower to fall,
To pierce façade and rampart through and through,
Into the deepest hideaway to crawl.
Where sacred silence reigned, begin to brew
Quarrel and discord, swelling to a brawl,
In happy, torpid minds evoking rabies,
Stirring the monks who had lazed sweetly as babies.

Father Hilary, awakened by the sound,
Bearishly vexed, grumbled, 'What's going on!?'
The Prior, too, blinking from bed of down,
For the first time in years beheld the dawn.
The thickest cushion availed not to drown
The frightful din; so soon the cloister Don
— Damning too-healthy ears — in angry haste
Left book and bed, and into refectory raced.

At such a sight, the brothers who had grouped
Beneath clay steins of beer there, knelt in fright;
Behind the Don tumbled another group
Of brothers — 'twas as if their panicked flight
Had been a sport, they jostled so and swooped;
The monk then set his pouch and hood aright,
Sat on the bench (beneath his girth it groaned)
And in such splendid terms, his verdict he intoned:

'Beloved brothers! Wherefore comes this din?
Whence comes this riot, ne'er before seen here?

Check out the pantry! Have thieves broken in?
Or have we clean run out of wine and beer?
Whatever's sparked this tumult that you're in,
Speak up! and soon the murky air will clear!'
He spoke, he choked, he coughed, and he teared up,
At which the Prior hastened to fill full his cup.

While he was pondering what next to say,
A quick glance at the cup the doctor takes;
Vodka, it was, flavoured with caraway,
And next to it, some Toruń ginger-cakes,
Slathered with sugar frosting; golden they lay
(The kind of gift that prioresses make).
The Prior urged him, 'Please, most reverend sir,
For stamina!' Nor did the doctor long demur.

O! Rarely met with, gift of eloquence!
Who can resist Thy overmastering pow'r?
To such urgings, the Don had no defence.
Lifting the cup (in the sweat of his brow)
He swigged it down — to replenish his strengths;
Then, to make sure they'd not be flagging now
(The monks were hanging on his every word),
He took a second draught, and (just in case) a third.

Just as, after the long and gloomy night
The sky blushes with gladness at the dawn,
The dew fills drooping flowers with new might;
They grow erect as the warm sun moves on
About the sky, with just such brisk delight,
After his cordials, the doctor's eyes shone:
He cleared his throat and smiled, thoroughly pleased,
Blinked twice his puffy lids, swelled out his chest, and sneezed.

Upon this signal, all the legions bright
Of fathers, ranked by station and decree,
Cried out at once a heartfelt 'Gesundheit!'
In grave canonical antiphony.

Then Father Honoratus, who by right
Was most esteemed of the whole company,
The Holy Rosary's famed champion,
Rose to his feet to speak, these words upon his tongue:

'Chrysippus once wrote of King Alfonzo
That, waging war against the Bactrians,
He was separated from his men, and so
Found that he'd been surrounded on all hands.
Athirst, he drank of the Pactolan flow.
This so revived his strengths, he slew the bands
Of pagans pressing him. Thus it is writ:
Pereat umbra! Lemma of great worth and wit!

'As great Tostado writes, it's clear to see —
The dark night passes into the bright day.
When virtue's coupled with meet majesty,
True happiness cannot be far away.
What need we fear, brothers, catastrophe?
With such a man to lead us in this fray,
The learned doctor — of whom none is bolder;
Thus, lift your hearts on high! Onward, Christian soldiers!'

Finished, he sat. Father Gaudenty then
(After a tipple) felt his spirits rise.
In testimony to his great chagrin
He blinked his bleared, still puffy-with-sleep eyes
And said, 'If there be any, brethren,
Who sin by turning cheeks, it is not I.
The sad clouds of dissent which round us hover,
Whence come they, ask you? This I shall now uncover.

'The root of all these broils is jealousy,
Which in the wreck of innocents delights;
Invidious of our prosperity,
From caverns dank it crawls into the light.
Whence this miasma? From the Carmelites!
And no less from the sons of Augustine!

Trust not those who connive behind our back.
It's time we pooled our strengths, and rushed to the attack!'

Father Pankracy, a Nestor wise and hoary,
Who told more beads than all the monks combined,
Bowed to the elders and brothers, before he
Set loose his tongue and by sweet words inclined
Their minds and hearts with gentle oratory.
In such terms did the old man speak his mind:
'Consider, brothers — by this silver hair —
For ancients to utter vain words, 'tis passing rare.

'How long it's been since first I took my place
A novice in these stalls! And in that time
I've come to know well men of all estates,
Both lay and regular, and can testify:
Neither cowl nor habit offers sure escape
From envy's barb and ill-will's dart malign;
Though one have wisdom, dignity to spare,
Let him always be on his guard — always beware!

'O my dear brethren! if you only knew
The way things were when I, like you, was young!
Monks acted otherwise than now they do;
Greater the men were; greater deeds were done!
Degenerate this age is, through and through —
So dull and lazy have we monks become:
When this one courage, that one prudence lacks,
And no one weighs consequences before he acts!

'As matters stand then, I insist we must
Challenge our rivals to a clash of wits.
They'll come to know our arms are free of rust;
They'll beg for mercy as they call it quits,
And as they grovel, supine in the dust,
Their bitter penance shall be to admit
Our victory, as we in laurels crowned
Tread down the wretches, like our forefathers renowned.'

He ended. In relief, the Prior groaned,
The Don awoke, the Lector rubbed his eyes;
Brother Makary, old and deaf as stone,
Seeing the lips grow still did softly rise
To skip back to his cell, while Ildefons
Bucked like a colt loosed from oppressive guys.
Then Morpheus, their tender-hearted sire,
Sifted sleep upon his children, which they most desired.

Canto II

Contents

The unpropitious accident of Father Raymund causes consternation within the walls of Carmel. The fathers gather together just as envoys from the sons of Dominic arrive to challenge them to a disputation.

    The early sun blushed rose the eastern horizon
    As in their coops the hens began to cackle.
    Throughout the monastery monks were rising,
    While at the gate milled the devoted gaggle
    Of dames; there Father Raymund rushed, surmising
    He'd set his ear to their moral tongue-waggle.
    Sunk deep in thoughts (on things divine? Who knows?)
    He caught his sandal, tripped, and fell down on his nose.

    Good Father Raymund was a learned soul,
    And so he saw in this a gloomy sign.
    At once the cloister bells began to toll,
    Which but deepened his forebodings malign.
    He sat there in a funk, while dark thoughts rolled
    Hither and thither through his worried mind;
    Misfortune… passed? … Or yet to come? … Which is it?
    When his friend from the next cell paid him a visit.

    'Twas Father Rafał of the Flesh Divine —
    Faithful companion of his blameless joys;
    Another such in Carmel you won't find
    Amongst its ribald and fresh, smooth-cheeked boys;
    Seeing his friend sprawled low, perturbed, the kind
    Lad knelt, concerned: 'I thought I heard a noise!

Poor Father Raymund! Friend! Are you all right?
What's wrong? Your nose! You're trembling! O, you look a fright!'

'Alas, my friend! In misfortune begun,
Unlucky will unfold this fatal day!
"The first step sets the paths the planets run"
Is what I've heard the wisest prophets say.
Nothing can change what Destiny has spun —
I rose, I ran, I fell — and here I lay!
An evil sign — catastrophe awaits!
Today's no day for gossip at the dear cloister gates!'

He spoke, and broke down sobbing. Then came word
That 'Madame Dorota waits for you outside.'
Raymund made no reply. A second, third
Note came… One worried, and another one to chide…
'Get up!' said Rafał, 'These fears are absurd!
You mustn't shunt our patroness aside —
Conquer your superstition! Break its hold!
Courage! They also say: "Fortune favours the bold!"'

With pain he rises, but, as strong sea-walls
Repulse the billows of the fiercest seas,
No sooner does he reach the porch — he falls,
And moans, and strains, and… weeps upon his knees.
Rafał still cheers him, but in vain, his pleas,
No matter how he threatens, urges, calls.
Seeing how fruitless is his oratory,
He summons the elders, and the definitory.

In rushes Elias of St Barbara,
With Mark of the Holy Trinity in his train,
And John of St Peter de Alcántara
And Hermenegildus of the Seven Pains,
Rafał of Peter, Peter of St Clara…
Hardly a patroned monk without remains.
Both old and young group round, both pale and ruddy:
All ranks and dignities; in short: everybody.

The reverend prior soon began to quack
(So nasal was his voice). He'd but begun…
When Father Mark in boredom turned his back,
Spinning his scapular about his thumb,
And Father Blaise each of his knuckles cracked;
Old Eli was by slumber overcome.
Some monks a hasty exit soon contrived,
But then the white hooded emissaries arrived.

First was Gaudenty, he of widespread fame,
Who'd test the fates by being first to fight.
Sworn enemy of tricks and clever games,
Bristling with vigour, certain of his might.
With wit pugnacious he could entertain,
With hand, not pen, always in graceful flight;
Sublime of eye, stately, complexion clear;
In short: a hero, knowing neither doubt, nor fear.

His second was the youthful Hyacinth,
Of lofty lowliness, splendid in modesty;
Of cloistered sisters the great favourite
(Excepting Rafał), slim, of great beauty,
His cowl — ah, wanton winds toyed with it
As through the sacred halls on dancer's foot he
Glided; those two, then — one pretty, one wise,
Delivered the message as they'd been deputised.

Gaudenty first the Carmelites did greet:
'Good fathers, now's the time the world to show
Who has the better claim to wisdom's seat;
Whose academic deeds more brightly glow.
If Carmel's cells with books are yet replete,
And Learning, like an outcast, does not go
Amongst you pining, come to a dispute —
Though ours will be to triumph, and yours, to rue it.'

Then Hyacinth coughed (thrice; and twice he smiled)
Before he spoke in his turn. 'My dear friends,

Dear fathers, deign our mission with a mild
Ear to receive, for we mean no offence;
Should I convince you to this learned trial
— And this the sum of our order's intents —
With joy unbounded would my bosom swell
For having found such grace in glorious Carmel.

'As midst oppressive heat — refreshing shade,
Our order craves your reverent regard,
To show you what advances we have made
In learning; thus, a friendly battle-sward
We call you to, where wit will be displayed
In gentle combat; beneath the pauldron hard
A tender heart beats: seeking only merry
Confrontation, with a worthy adversary.'

He finished — then charm yielded to unease
When in the monks' minds it began to dawn:
What's this? A duel of philosophies?
The muttering grew, and most would fain be gone
From danger; nothing smiled now but Gaudenty's
Eyes as a growing chaos they looked on.
But then the prior, (of highest eminence there)
Arose, and to both envoys thus did he declare:

'With willing hearts your gauntlet we pick up.
Appoint the place, the hour — we'll appear.
Forces for such a war we've quite enough,
And weapons — sharp still — of that, have no fear.
Your brazen words will find a bold rebuff
And who shall rue the fight is far from clear.
He totters not, whose feet are firmly set;
We're neither flattered by your songs, nor fear your threats.'

Gaudenty swelled to pay him back with fire
For such bold speech, but Hyacinth took pains
To temper with sweet words his seething ire;
So that their legation should not be stained,

He pushed him out the door, and then retired,
Bidding the monks farewell, in gentler vein.
Soon they regained the cloister courtyard, where
They made the gate, without loss of a single hair,

Whilst Carmel was plunged into fresh ferment —
Father Makary sees no point in strife;
Father Cherubin cites a precedent.
Father Seraphin calls for drum and fife;
Father Pafnucy counsels spies be sent;
Father Elias likes the quiet life.
Some fear, while some would spring to foeman's throat;
And Father Zephyrin even declines to vote.

The wronger side oft carries the debate.
Here too, the martial party swelled, and won.
The undecided opt to test their fate
And soon defensive measures are begun.
Young passions wax; mature counsels abate,
And no one hears the chimes for sext or nones.
Then Brother Cleophas rings the dinner bell,
And all race to the tables, like bats out of Hell.

Canto III

Contents

The Carmelites take counsel concerning the coming debate. Brothers are sent forth in search of the library, which they find in the attic. One and all set to reading. The sons of Dominic are shown in similar preparations.

Thoughts sharpen on a strict diet of bread
And water? Thus taught the fanatic sage…
Well, fool us once… Today's scholars are bred
According to the mores of this age,
In which fasting and measure nigh are dead.
Gravy and wine stain even the wiseman's page,
Whose brains are fortified with mead and beer,
And sunny wine refills the gloomy heart with cheer.

This truth was confirmed by the reverend fathers,
Who set their feet upon the well-trod way
Of wisdom (this one firmly, that one totters),
Brimming with joy (and drink — their hearts made gay)
To fresh debate (so gay, no one is bothered
By reprised confabs — each has something to say!)
Father Gervase of the Annunciation
Was the first to offer his sober oration.

'And so we've had our fill; we've drunk and dined;
Our quandaries, good fathers, yet remain.
Will we be bested in debate? I find
It's better to keep honour free from stain,
Inviting them here, and drinking them blind.
Then we shall see who's got the stouter brain!

We'll conquer them, and all the world will see
How hearts of oak bear up under adversity!'

Father Hilary next: 'Be not so bold!
Seek not, good brother, to provoke such arms.
Heed well your elders, who've seen knights of old
(Ah, age heroic!) face fiercer alarms
Than those you threaten. Chalices of gold
No brandy softens, be it ne'er so warm.
I, and Antoni, know them well. As able
As you may be, they'll drink you under the table!'

Nine other voices amplified the fray
On either side, till Father Eli's turn
Came round. 'I've heard all that you've had to say,
For and against. A righteous zeal burns
Within me; though reluctant — if I may —
With heavy heart I say it: I discern
Our age of gold is gone for good. It looks
As if we must set mugs aside, and reach for... books!

'And who's to blame for this? The king! Indeed —
'Tis he who promotes this modish temperance,
Who scorns wine, beer, and has no taste for mead;
Nor will he lift a finger in defence
Of brewer or vintner in their urgent need;
Whose only interest books are! And science!
Who's never soared aloft by vodka fuelled,
Must keep us dry and grounded too? Alas! Too cruel!

'Thus, we must hit the books. Now, ancient lore,
Passed down by generations of our kind,
Declares that, somewhere, we've a hefty store
Of books, patiently waiting for the time
Someone shall crack them open. It's been more
Than thirty years since Alphonse had a mind
To broach the — what d'you call it? — library
Up in the rafters; it's high time we go and see

'What's to be found there; perhaps something of use?
Even the slightest bucklers can protect.'
He spoke, but all fell silent. Each refused
To undertake the hazards of the trek;
Each had a fitting, readymade excuse
To shun the deed. At last the monks elect
Two gentle, backward souls to search the nooks
And crannies for those fabled creatures known as — books.

Between the bell tower and a weedy plot
Upon which an old bastion's ruins lay,
Sagged an old outbuilding eaten through by rot,
Whose roof-beams even the slightest breeze would sway.
Pedestrians gave a wide berth to the spot,
Where death might pounce on any given day.
And yet, 'tis there we find our doughty team
Of book-hunters, braving decayed joint, crumbling beam.

Intrepid souls! who threats and peril mock,
And pass on to the goal! Theirs was a door —
Massive and iron-bound. Pausing to take stock
Of this obstacle, which but whetted the more
Their resolution — they tried out the lock:
It gave at once ('twas rusted to the core),
The door creaked open; their eyes were cheered to see
Great treasures: the worm-eaten, mouldy library.

Meanwhile, Dominic's prior, quaffing beer
(To calm his nerves) was startled and nearly choked
By a herald from the mission who burst clear
And sudden through his door. 'Your grace!' he spoke…
'Damn it!' the prior cursed, taken unawares
(He'd jumped so, that the ale his habit soaked)
But, at the news, his anger turned to joy:
After a swig (for penance) he treated the envoy.

Ah, joys of the fermented grape and grain!
Who pines not for you? Young or old, well or

Sick — for you they'll endure the aching brain;
Because of you, cheery the darkest cellar;
You banish sadness, soothe longing and pain;
You profit both your buyer and your seller:
No toil so great, too sore no deprivation
If but to plunge, at last, into inebriation.

Enough digressions. What the Blackfriars found
Amongst the lees, jealous time now bars
From close inspection. See the doctor, bound
To seek the nuns' advice; alas, not ours
The ears to hear what wit reserved resounds
In the confessional… Well then, so far:
The monks now set their flasks and cups apart,
And take to tome and quarto — with less than soaring heart.

For look: the doctor is returning now,
Of quizzing nun and abbess he's had his fill.
The monks — as faithful to him as to their vows —
Entrust themselves completely to his will.
He orders all the cloister gates locked. How
Sober now the sacred halls! How still!
The clink of glass and laughter fade, and all,
Even Gaudenty, are knee-deep in rubricals.

Just as when Jove the clouds of heaven drums
With thunder, ere the first sharp bolt is hurled,
And Atlas, startled at the chaos, jumps
(Beneath his heavy feet quakes the whole world)
From Vulcan's forge resound the hammer-thumps
And sparks above his hill crackle and swirl,
So here. A din to astonish the ages:
The air's filled with the sound of monks… turning pages!

O haven, once, of blest simplicity!
What anguish now uproots their happiness?
You! Wretched books! *Virtuous industry.*
Has it a place in realms of blissfulness?

Must theological controversy
Deprive two reverend orders of their rest,
And jealousy, vengeance, pique and envy sore
Lash brethren vowed to peace, into the maw of war?

Canto IV

Contents

The learned men congregate for the disputation. The Lord Vicegerent shall act as Maecenas. After a few arguments sallied and parried, a shouting match ensues, followed by chaos and fisticuffs.

O! You, whom no one's ever understood,
No matter how long he should rack his brains,
Lost in your writings, as in a dense wood,
Still praising you, though he would strive in vain
To clarify — if ever mortal could! —
Your wisdom, obscure Aristotle! Deign,
Scholastic god, accept my altar's smoke,
Thick as the oxen's polls, that strain beneath your yoke!

Sometimes the ass parades in lion's skin;
A pretty woman's child can look a fright.
Tall cedars oft sprout saplings dwarfed and thin;
Tares steal within, strong fields of corn to blight.
And if your progeny are as dumb as sin,
That's not your fault. And bastards have no right
To claim inheritance — not by a half!
Look down upon these trifles of mine, and laugh.

And so the sages gather: grey and white,
The black, the tan, discalced and sandal-shod;
With boldness are their blushing faces bright;
Above their heads distends thick, learned fog
The while their eyes shine with envy and pride.
Only one order won't be over-awed:

Meek always, everywhere, here they retire
To the dim depths, and no one says, 'Friends, come higher!'

Cineas thought them kings in majesty,
When he beheld the Roman senators;
Thus you seem, masters of theology,
You bachelors, and regents, and lectors,
And you, above all in sublimity,
Provincials, generals, definitors!
As lightning o'er the Tatras before the storm,
So flashes of wisdom above your tonsures swarm.

Now came the Vicegerent, and all arose.
Wise, prudent, fair, a man of wide renown,
In coat of marten, scarlet were his shoes.
He took his place, then all the rest sat down.
The rector next (in alb of lynx he goes)
Then the *Proponens* come, with a smug frown.
The *Defendens* stood, when all were in their place,
And in such wise began his oration: 'Your Grace,

'The ark of wisdom, sad, frustrated, moors
Useless, when tide is out, in barren shallows.
It needs a thunderous runoff from the sewers
To lift it from the mire where it wallows
And set it on its way; thus we need yours,
Your Grace — your wit, which each here hallows,
As our bound reason's surest emetic;
You, pearl in the crown of the Peripatetic!

'The sun, whose radiance the whole cosmos warms;
The planets, which apportion night and day;
The moon, that now displays, now hides its horns;
The stars that make the gloomy nighttime gay;
All these we find upon your coat of arms —
Seal of a clan deserving royal sway!
Of prince and margrave the ever bubbling fount,
That makes Tarnowski, Górka, and Krasicki, count.

'Silence, ye Bourbons! Or in novel tones
Sing the renown wherewith Sarmatia teems!
And you, descendants of the Jagiellons,
And you, Ausonian Guelphs and Ghibellines,
Pour forth your hymns in praise of deeds well done
By our Vicegerent — let them flow in streams
And bear unto the distant generations
The glories wherewith his scutcheon is emblazoned!

'Let Zoilus swell with envy and drop dead!
Let Syrta and Charybdis disappear!
Let Pactolus seek a new fountain-head,
Olympus and Parnassus quake in fear!
The planets six scan *your* motions instead,
O, Glory of our land! Our nation's Cheer!
Atlas, to you, 's a dwarf — the Sphinx, a pixie,
Centaur and Bucentaur, mere puppies! *Dixi*.'

He sat, and silence fell. Until up stirred
Reverend Father Łukasz of Three Kings.
Foregoing flowery term and learned word,
Leaving Duns and Bartolus in the wings
(To Hydaspes he might well have referred,
But why muddy the waters with such things?)
Casting upon his foe a brazen eye,
He strung his bow with dart *Baroque*, and let it fly.

If not for the *Distinguo's* trusty shield,
By the first shot the *Defendens* were slain.
But gracefully the buckler did he wield,
The dart deflecting. To rebuttal fain,
He gripped a missile, braced on his back heel,
Then the *Oppugnans* shot at him again!
'Twas a *celarent*, as from crossbow sped,
But weakly aimed, so, harmless, it flew past his head.

Twice rescued, see the hero fresh beset
With all the fury of a third assault.

His dart unquivered barely had been set
Against the tendon, which he then drew taut,
When a great cry apprised him of a threat
Among his comrades — where no one had thought
A general melée was to break out,
And yet: fists flew, trumps pealed, drums rolled — in short, a rout.

All who were scrapping not, astonished, froze.
Even the Maecenas (despite his girth)
Panting, to quell the pandemonium, rose
And cried in a loud voice for all his worth:
'Gentlemen! Please! It needn't come to blows!'
Yet no one heeded, tumbling over the earth;
Even the doctor quaked — as did the hall,
Such was the chaos; Were the heavens about to fall?

Sweet Hyacinth, who rather was intent
On paying court to the Vicegerent's wife,
Stopped short, midcourse of his next compliment.
Distracted by the loud, intrusive strife,
He dropped the cup of wine with which he'd meant
To drink her health. Poor Brother Czesław dived
To save the liquor — alas, it stained her silk
Voluptuous frock (and other items of that ilk).

On the monks' battle raged. Hyacinth stroked
And rubbed the lady's lap until he'd dried
The dampness, then, into her ear he spoke
Some gentle words, and so they drew aside
To some place meditative, and remote
From tumults; alas, neither time nor tide
Waits on man's will, or woman's entreaty,
Fleeting most swiftly at moments of ecstasy…

Now, she'd a figure full of grace; her eyes,
Half-closed in prayer, at times would flash with flame;
A fetching lisp (although her words were pious),
Dressed modestly (yet such a minxy frame

Reveals itself to each who barely tries
His fancy) in short: she'd mastered the game.
The while she fingered her beads, piously humming,
Hyacinth mused of a different second coming.

'Twas not with thin romances that she fed her
Sweet intellect, not vampire, ghoul, nor wraith;
She read Erasmus, discoursed on d'Agreda
(Her Gothic was pure — of the Age of Faith.)
To hear her scourge sin, you'd have thought her dead, or
Cold to delight, but then, in the next breath,
You caught a… soupçon… of impropriety;
The way she teased, she'd slay a man with piety.

To such a swelling head she'd rubbed the quat —
Poor Hyacinth! Near swooning with delight,
When rumours of the battle reached this spot
Secluded, and filled the poor monk with fright.
Of all things, a bold brawler he was *not*.
He leapt to his feet, determined to take flight.
'Stay, Hyacinth!' in vain, the lady's tears;
In vain the efforts of Czesław, who'd brought some beers…

Three times did Hyacinth lunge for the door;
Three times the lady's arms did him restrain.
At last, he tore loose; she fell to the floor
As he escaped, in quite a comely faint.
(There Czesław left her. Frankly, he cared more
For beer than any young seductive saint.)
Meanwhile, through hill and dale, Hyacinth sped,
Through cobbled street and gutter; chivvied by Fate, he fled.

Canto V

Contents

The battle. Father Gaudenty is conspicuous in heroic deeds. The Rector, Vicegerent and Doctor confer on how to bring the conflict to an end. At last, they decide upon introducing the vitrium gloriosum.

Laughter too can be, shall we say, didactic —
When at men's foibles, not themselves, it's aimed;
If witty are the jokes, and nothing drastic,
Like love-taps (they may sting, but will not lame).
Thus criticism, even if emphatic,
Like a physician, should heal, not maim.
Let's treat the patterns of the wise as rules,
While laughing at all stupid, though reverend, fools.

And thus we come back to the holy war,
As did Hyacinth (worry besting fear).
What meets his eyes? Scrums fearsome, thwackings sore
(Even our sweet knight caught one full on the ear!)
That got him riled! Indebted, he'd not for-
Give his debtors; grabbing what was near
(Two cowls, each with a head within) the meek
Monk smashed them; so much for turning the other cheek!

He'd split two tonsures, cursing still the day
When brethren first took up uncivil arms.
Sandals and friar's cords around him lay,
And breviaries flew about his head in swarms.
Once more he sought somehow to slip away,
Somewhere, to give, nor to receive, more harms,

But just as from the battlefield he stole,
A well-aimed mug from Father Zephyrin laid him low.

Gaudenty roared in pain like lion pierced
When he beheld Hyacinth on the ground.
Tearing through the melée in ire fierce,
Dispensing angry cudgels all around,
He knocked the Maecenas heels over ears,
Un-cowled the rector, then began to pound
The definator with some sturdy clouts;
Łukasz crumpled; Kleofas' last two teeth were knocked out.

The screams and shouts of war fly through the hall.
Here, one curls foetally, there someone bleeds;
Father Remigius, sinewy and tall,
Swings with ruthless precision his heavy beads.
Capistran, brained by barrel, swooning, falls;
Dydak fells Symphorus with mug of mead.
Like viper hissing, Regulat pins his man,
While Longinus, sword-like, brandishes frying pan.

The cups all smashed, and all the trenchers split
(The thicker pates shattered even stout beer steins)
Gaudenty seized a tome of Holy Writ.
This in his grip, he decimated the lines
Of knights opposing him, nor would he quit
Till all had tasted of its well-bound spine.
Thus once in Palestine, that famed hero passed,
Slaying Philistines with the jawbone of an ass.

This seeing, Raymund, Carmel's ornament,
Dominic's son in triumph can't abide.
He plunges straight into the moil, intent
On stemming this advancing bloody tide.
Gaudenty seems a worthy opponent
(Especially with Rafał at his side)
'To me, lad!' the words had barely left his mouth
When, brained with hagiography, he was knocked out.

At this, Rafał felt tears rush to his eyes.
Too late he learns to credit prophecy!
Why must misfortune always make us wise?
But then uprose before him Gaudenty!
Swiftly he grasps aspergill; in a trice
He bonks Gaudenty on the nut. And he,
Expecting not the sudden holy shower,
Stood wet, astonished, abstracted from his power.

But then he shook it off; cleared now, his head,
He set about his task with doubled vigour.
Father Barnabas — better lie abed
Than play at war and valour, don't you figure?
And you, Paphnutius? Better to have fled
Back to your cell and meditative rigour
Like old Gervais, who, fear-struck, out of breath,
Sought to escape the clutches of this angel of death?

Thus, when from some exalted Alpine summit
A little stream from melted ice-drips grows
And gathers strength the longer that it plummets,
Boring its way through granite as it goes,
Booming afar like baleful, angry comet,
Sweeping whole forests in among its floes
Foaming and dealing ruin on each hand,
The more powerful, the longer it's been dammed,

So is armed conflict. How to put an end
To all this internecine thuggery?
The Vicegerent consults the rector: 'Friend,
What is it monks desire most?' 'Well, b...'
                    'Brown-juggery!'
Breaks in the doctor. 'Excellent! Let's send
For the Bottle!' Among the hugger-muggery,
They pick their way, cautious and ever heedful,
In search of a panacea, that is, The Needful.

As was in Troy the idol of Athena,
As was for Rome the sacred vestal flame,
Amongst the friars was held in such esteem a
Bottle of ancient liquor. No profane
Dared e'er approach its shelf, on which, serene, a
Flickering light, like chancel lamp in fane
Hierophanic amidst the tuns did glow,
Save Father Sexton, first doing obeisance low.

Who more than he deserved the august role
To keep the bottle, cherish, and protect?
Who better knew the merit of ancient bowl
And cup? None other bore the hallowed object
In peace or war processing, but he, sole,
Before the novices, who'd genuflect.
Even the trumpeter, from his aerie proud
Would descend his steeple, to bow with the awed crowd.

'Twas this they sent for, and before too long
The solemn conduct set out for the fray.
With reverent applause and joyful song
The urn was greeted all along the way
Until it rested amidst the awestruck throng
Of battling monks, whose arms all fell away
From hands clasped piously, while Father Sexton,
Unsure at first, regained his ruddy complexion.

For though his sense of duty trumped his fear,
The sight of the Vicegerent's worried face
Seemed a bad sign of what transpired here;
And as they made their passage through the gates
The tokens dire of war were all too clear.
Still, all did homage as the jug of grace
Was borne aloft amongst the strife-scarred friars
Until they reached the doctor's cell, where they retired.

Canto VI

Contents

The jug described. The treasures graven thereon: the graces and recreations of the four seasons. Soon, everyone sets their weapons aside in presence of the brimful vessel, and happy concord succeeds upon the battle.

And so, dear fathers, with this song we end!
I beg your patience, please — we're almost done.
Where there's a critic, there's one to defend…
Recall this, if you're miffed: It's all in fun;
Why be angry? You've heard that learned men
Have stains discovered even on the sun?
Well, whether we wield crozier, hoe or pike,
Our natures, and our shortcomings, are all alike.

The jug was set in a conspicuous place
Where it the warring legions might behold.
All eyes were wonderstruck at its rare grace:
With silver was it chased, and graven gold.
It was the jug of jugs! Eyebrows were raised
In awe at how much liquor it might hold!
An ornate tabernacle, with a frieze on
Its belly, showing the joys of all four seasons.

O happy spring! The skilful graver's hand
Your fresh delights upon the jug evoked:
See how the panting oxen plod the land,
Dredging the black earth, harnessed to the yoke.
The shepherd's pipings through the air expand,
Cheering the maids enwreathed, and simple folk

About their chores and pastimes innocent,
Amidst the budding boughs' intoxicating scent.

The squire comes, his faithful crew to greet,
Rejoicing in his fields in the late morn,
With wee grandchildren tumbling at his feet,
Exultant at the barely-sprouting corn.
He brings his workers lunch, and bids them eat;
They stretch out in the shade of the hawthorn.
Some young ones sing and dance, thumping the sod;
A priest looks on and smiles, praising the gifts of God.

And now the stalk is bent 'neath gravid ear,
The fledglings long ago have left their nests,
High summer brings her gifts as harvest nears,
And happy folk crowd to the parish fests.
Father Wojciech treats Pastor Martin to beer;
Peter and Luke drink deep, with all the rest
Of sextons on their off-day at the fair;
The busy kitchen helpers scurry here and there.

Autumn brings bumper crops: the oxen pull
Wagons piled high with sheavings of the scythe;
The squire's men shear the flocks of their thick wool
And fruit is canned, the winter to abide;
The squire grins: his granaries are full.
The priest grins also: happy with his tithe.
His smile grows broader with each day that passes,
As he computes his fees for baptisms and Masses.

Snow coats the fields as winter now begins,
Pinching the earth tight till the next warm spring.
But happy song sounds from the cheery inns
Where wit sharpens and faces flush with drink;
From door to village door the vicar wends
His way, with altar-boys a-carolling;
Gladly each hearth bids welcome to the priest;
Each pious visit ending with one toast… at least.

Above all this, such wondrous scenes unfold:
A flock of prelates all in chapter met,
Broad shoulders draped in pectorals of gold,
A festive board before their graces set;
Weary with labour, the pallium-clad fold
Was first blessed by the Dean, and then they ate.
Beneath them all — lurked Death, in the dark pantry;
Promising fulsome wake, and generous chantry.

All who are present, pause, their eyes to feast
Upon the jug. Even Caspar, (whose were black
And swollen with a thrashing). But now peace
Reigns, where wars raged, and all stand back
The while the doctor says his pacific piece:
'Lay down your clubs, and fill your mugs with sack!
Not throats fraternal, flagons should you throttle!'
The monks all shout 'Hip! Hip!' to the peace-making bottle.

Even misers rise to an emergency:
See Brother Czesław, fat, breath all but spent,
Trot up, toting fermented amity:
The stash he'd stored against lean days of Lent.
A toast he raises to His Excellency
That's seconded 'Hear, hear!' by all, content;
He passes the bottles round... with fists so tight,
The smiling doctor thinks upon the widow's mite.

Go now in peace and happiness, Fathers dear!
Go where fame leads you, in concord and love.
Where there is darkness, may your light shine clear;
May honour and men's praise forever rove
Before you and behind, and ever steer
You far from Aristotle. Give him a shove!
Be off, Peripatetic! For know this:
Your *quod ests* lead us... nowhere. Ignorance is bliss.

Now, into the refectory they bring
The jug (whence Mars Minerva first set to flight)

Where — groggy still — Raymond is seen to swing
His candelabra 'midst the boisterous fight.
'Put down your arms!' the doctor cries, the ring
Of tin on pewter stifling. The mere sight
Of the blest bottle fills the room with hushes,
Stilling all — save mad Gaudenty, who still rushes

About, thwacking, gouging, walloping, until
He hacks near to the treasure at the door,
Which stuns him with its numen. He grows still
And drops his bloody arms upon the floor.
All hail the sacred bottle, all are thrilled,
And sing out, 'Peace and concord! no more war!'
And whether black or white, or grey, or tan,
They're enemies no more: man loves his fellow man.

Whose name was sung then, by the toasting choir?
I don't know. I *do* know, if I were there,
It would be yours I'd drink to, worthy prior;
'Tis you, by dint of deed and virtue rare,
Raised to such heights to which few men aspire,
Who, both by learning and example fair
Teach your brethren, the greatest and the least
'Tis virtue, and not the collar, that makes the priest.

Read this my poem — and let them read it too,
Your brethren, for it's but a harmless jest.
There's nothing in it any ought to rue,
With blame or scandal feeling himself oppressed.
Censure taints virtue not, if it be true,
Wishing but vice to scold, when manifest.
If some page please you not, Father, then turn it;
You be my arbiter. Don't like my poem? Burn it.

END OF THE MONACHOMACHIA

ANTI-MONACHOMACHIA

Canto I

Contents

The book of the War of the Monks *falls into the hands of the Hag of Discord, and she promptly tosses it through the window of the doctor's cell. The sage man reacts to it with a smile, but Father Honoratus explodes in fierce anger, which the doctor strives to allay, in vain.*

Sometimes, appearances deceive the eyes,
Especially when overwrought, and weak —
Even the painter, who with passion tries
His canvas to perfect, the ideal to eke
From earthly stuff, no matter how he strives
— He's human! — can't avoid the odd mistake.
But, although mixed with dross, pure gold remains
Pure gold, proved by the flames — The dross? Away it drains.

O Hag of Discord! Such your evil tricks,
Whom petty acts of envy make to smile;
In art as well as science do you mix,
Spoiling happiness with your black bile,
For every itchy palm providing bricks;
With suchlike sport away your time you while;
Unslaked, your lust, with states' catastrophes:
You now take aim, with fatal dart, at monasteries?

Thus you determined, these sacred retreats
To tempt to vile contention yet again,
To try with new approach old treacheries,
Since your late half-success, this time to win,
— Vain thought! — o'er lamblike votaries
Protected by the righteous powers of Heaven!

But I shall sing, foul harpy spawned in Hell,
How once again, in confusion, conquered, you fell.

Sloth had no place in this monastery
Wherein she tried to sow her tragic seed;
Here was the pattern of integrity —
A cloister wide-famed for heroic deed,
The choice of all who sought true sanctity,
A granary of faith, where all did feed.
Blessed exemplar! Too feeble is my song
To hymn your praise aright, O fortress true, and strong!

A sacred prison that Love did erect,
Innocence ringed it round with bastions sure.
In this cloister, Zeal kept her abode elect,
Where Modesty made all within secure.
Beneath its shade Virtue was made perfect
And Faith defended from all that is impure.
At last! The candle atop the bushel rests!
A thaumaturge this cloister was, when all's confessed.

In such a refuge, than the Age of Gold
More worthy, pure sacrifice to God was raised,
Where Poverty and Obedience, as of old
Were honoured; Hope and Faith had pride of place;
Where tender Charity in good works was bold,
Winning a lavish recompense in grace;
There, Love was Virtue's active guarantor,
Sweetening labour on man's behalf, and the Lord's.

All this the hag of envy did abhor.
And thus she hatched her plan: at first, to find
Where was secreted the tome of the monks' war
— A harmless jest — for her harmful design:
To use it to enkindle a furore
Where none had felt her influence malign.
Alas! 'Twas not hid well enough; she crowed
With evil pleasure, fleeing with the baneful load.

Just as that apple, which kindled the row
'Twixt gods and men, was of the purest gold,
So this poor book — a harmless jest! — was now
Set to bad usage by a villain bold.
See her now soar above the abbey, to throw
The bomb of poison on the guileless fold!
The mere thought makes her laugh and clap her hands
And her miasma through the cloister halls expands.

Now at the doctor's door the hag of spleen
Lurks, thinking him deep in Somnus' arms at rest.
How wrong she was! For he was at compline,
The pious man, of all the monks the best;
There in the apse he knelt, at the rood screen
Lifting his voice in praise of the Highest.
By merit from such duty he's exempt;
By being there freely, greater his merit yet!

Inside his cell she crept. There in the gloom
She gasped — then groaned aloud in misery,
To see the cot of planks, the mat of broom,
All the signs of monastic poverty!
Books countless chocked the walls of the tight room —
Nowhere the slightest hint of luxury!
The humble tackle of the pious sage
Sent coursing through her arteries black floods of rage.

She tossed the screed, and with a frenzied yell
Returned from whence she came, with Jealousy,
Vengeance and fierce Fanaticism as well,
That holy precincts in confusion flee
For the familiar abysses of Hell —
Down to the springs of ghostly leprosy,
Whence to replenish her reserves of spleen,
The better to reprise her treacheries obscene.

The monk returned. And when he read the text,
He laughed — such the revenge of the grand soul.

Only the guilty are with anger vexed.
Who knows himself bad, in each evil role
Finds himself cast — only hypocrites
Fear their own shadows. He of conscience whole,
Untainted, innocent, has nought to rue;
He fears neither blame nor critic, whose virtue is true.

Like to a shoreline cliff, when weather looms
And in their black battalions mass the clouds,
The ocean heaves, the angry thunder booms,
And yet amidst the storm, unmoved, the proud
Cliff stands, as it will on the day of doom,
Though whitecaps pound the shore in frothy crowds,
And the winds shriek, impassive he, and grand —
The billows — lapdogs! — lick his feet firm on the sand.

Then Honoratus came to see his friend.
The smiling doctor handed him the screed…
No sooner had he the first strophe scanned
Than he turned livid. No more did he read;
He foamed, he would have torn it with his hands
Had not the doctor saved it, with all speed
Taking it back; the old priest growled and fumed,
Began to speak, choked on his anger, and resumed:

'Such the reward of our labours and pains?
Our prayers and fastings? Such ingratitude!
How boldly he jeers at wise men, and saints!
He spares neither father nor mother his rude
Fleerings; now at the rosary he aims
His bile-dipped pen? The scribe of Satan's brood!
If there's any spunk left in us, why, now
It's time for that blasphemer to know it — and how!

'The heretic! The Turk! The Jansenist!
An atheist, whom Hell's venom infects,
A libellous parasite, who profits
By casting broad his fellow man's defects!

May he be flung in shame's eternal pits,
He and all those who follow in his steps!
May he be...' here anathemas ran dry
In the riled priest's throat, to whom the doctor made reply:

'It misbecomes the pious, in their zeal
To curse, whose office rather is, to bless.
Venom makes wounds the worse. It cannot heal!
Will empty bellowings win us redress?
Vengeance his friends to God does not reveal.
Vengeance is His, should He deem fit to press
The charge. Though pain may bore unto the soul,
To suffer, and be silent — this is the monk's role.

'He, Who on our behalf took up the Cross
Counselled us to repay evil with good.
One hundred-fold He can redeem our loss;
Revenge won't win a mite. It never could!
Patience will bring to sorest smartings pause
If we follow our Master, as we should...
Forgive —' But Honoratus, full of wrath,
Stormed off. Alas! Sometimes the seed falls on the footpath...

He might scold him, as his superior.
But he was old; despite that flaming rage,
With each day's toil, Honoratus grew wearier,
With all infirmities befitting age;
The doctor's disposition was much cheerier:
Willing, where works were found, to impute faith;
Where he saw error, the errant's integrity
Moved him to pardon, in pious simplicity.

Canto II

Contents

Honoratus causes an uproar in the cloister with his cries and laments. He storms into the library, upsetting four lecterns, along with their books. Then he retails a long catalogue of his complaints, to which the librarian makes reply.

Like a storm cloud that rolls above the fields,
Honorat races through the cloister halls;
Like an alarm bell that frantically peals
When fire erupts, thus his alarms he calls,
'Justice!' (that is, for vengeance he appeals,
Condemning author, work, genre, and all
That irks him): 'To me! Help! Help! Here, my friends!
We've been attacked! Come! To the common weal's defence!'

At such a clamour, as if lightning-struck,
The friars toss labour and sport aside.
Their habit-folds high in their cords they tuck
And hasten in large crowds from far and wide
To Honoratus. Full of concern, they'd pluck
His flagging spirits, but the more they tried
To comfort him, their brother sore beset,
They but succeeded in making him madder yet.

Just like the deer that wanders the deep glade,
Fawn at her side — her tender nature's care,
When by misstep to hunter is betrayed
Will fly, to flee the pain, her life to spare —
But though she slip his snare, at length she's laid
Low by the fatal dart that's ever there,

A pain she can't outrun, deep in her side,
Her woe and frenzy growing, never to subside,

He screams, he froths, he howls; no soothing pleas
Can calm the outrage of the frenzied chap,
Cut to the quick of honour and prestige.
O self-esteem! Is there a snider trap
For righteous souls? He wrestles loose, and flees
Into the library, where, as it happed,
The door gaped open. In the old man, burning
With wrath, speeds, lecterns four (and books) overturning.

O Thou, who of all sages, understand
Fair nature best, the Lord's own translator,
Who most deserves the praise of every man;
Thou sweetly-teaching wiseman, educator,
Pearl of all writers, Thou, Albert the Grand,
Of deepest mysteries swift explicator,
Thou too wast basely from pulpit knocked down,
And with thy fellows lain, sprawled on the dusty ground!

Tostado! Who with wisdom and aplomb
Wrote about… well, wrote about everything…
You too were cast from cathedra ere long
By anger — such as from holy zeal springs —
But, seeing you amidst the clutter flung,
Sorrow from the priest's eyes hot tears did wring,
As if you'd been pummelled by that barbarian.
In tears then, the old man addressed the librarian:

'Not only men and books does he insult,
The godless boor, who raised impious hand
Against the monks! What was Tostado's fault?
What King Alfonso's, that beloved man?
In bold pasquilles the blind mocker exults,
Warping the ancient legends of the land!
Unworthy lout! Imagine what great harm he'd
Do to *Fresh Recruits to the Tender-Hearted Army!*

'I know from whence arises all such bile:
The world's gone bad; its fruit ripens to rot.
They cast their venom with the sweetest smile,
Those *philosophes* — whose names shall be forgot!
Such are their concepts, their mendacious style.
But we'll fight them as they've never been fought!
They don't know who they're grappling with this time!
That hack and his screed will soon drown in their own slime.

'Would that the first book never had been brought out!
In the old days, everyone just kept quiet!
What of the new discoveries they've sought out?
Is the world jot or tittle better by it?
Our fathers weren't like these moderns caught out:
When they said something, even should they write it,
They never saw in wisdom cause to brag,
Nor soiled their hands with printed book, or scandal rag!'

'More than one dunce has found his way to print,'
Said the librarian to Honoratus.
'Print neither signifies ennoblement
Nor rubbish. Time's wheels turn as turn they must;
The stupid and the wise in permanent
And varied gavotte parade before us.
No better we, nor worse, than those of old:
In our days too one can be a sage, or a dolt.

'And so he laughs at our simplicity.
Let's laugh as well! Heap hot coals on his head.
He'll see by how we laugh he was too free —
And wrong, too. He'll retract all that he said.
What will we win through rage and enmity?
We'll only make his venom worse. Instead,
Met halfway, he'll not just cease to enerve us,
Perhaps, horns lowered, he'll even come to serve us.'

'Fine service that! Pasquilles, satires and gibes!'
'Please, Father Honoratus — let me talk.

You just don't know the customs of that tribe.
Rhymers the wildest fancies will concoct;
It sometimes haps that inspiration drives
Them to a witty turn that seems to mock,
When laughter, and not slander, was their aim.'
'Evil the laughter that feeds another's pain!'

'The pasquille preys on trembling innocence,
Infects with venom, joys to vandalise,
But satire can abide no pestilence;
Respects no rank, sets vice before our eyes.
With zeal — not unlike yours — checked by prudence —
Gaily, not meanly, critics criticise.
Such is their art, the rules of which are fair:
Folly to excoriate, but persons to spare.'

'But he attacked me!' 'Mere coincidence!'
'Coincidence? He mocked my advanced years!'
'In person? I suppose there's a slight chance.
But had he you in mind? That's far from clear.
How have we been defamed, good Father, since
What he expressed — It didn't happen here!
Such witty sallies no man ever minds
Unless… within himself, a grain of truth he finds.

'Mere hazard, that he chanced to use your name.
His Honoratus isn't him we know.
Are you as stubborn as an ass gone lame?
Which brother finds in you a bitter foe?
Who calls you lazy? Who has ever blamed
You for a drunk, to books and matins slow?
You're good! You're wise! Prone to divine afflatus!
That screed's nothing to do with our Honoratus!'

'Beautiful words, but they don't mean a thing!'
Roared the old priest, 'He mocked us to our face!
Such apologias have a fishy ring
When they defend so wanton a scapegrace.

His words of mockery hurt, I say! They sting,
No matter what a modern wiseman says.
God help us all now! For I fear I suss
A modern tilt in you too, Father Boniface!'

Canto III

Contents

The hag awakens the sleeping Gaudenty, stirring his bile. Rising from his cot, he runs out, and comes upon Father Honoratus. After hearing the latter's complaints concerning the dishonour done to the religious life, he determines to use all means to take revenge upon the calumniator.

To sleep! To sleep! A slumber deep and mild,
Whether on down or plank, the nap we're taking,
To sleep! Perchance to dream! Even when wild,
A dream bests all the woe we see when waking;
Though crazy, still by dreams I'd be beguiled.
So sweet, sometimes with joy they leave you aching!
In sleep, each moment flows delightfully —
Though careworn kings sleep not, 'tis not so with Gaudenty.

Untroubled conscience! Such is thy great gift:
Of honest toil delightful interlude,
The strength that labour from our bodies strips
Through gracious sleep thou giv'st back, renewed.
Though into fitful drowse the lazy drift,
Unsatisfied they wake in cranky mood —
Not thus Gaudenty. Deep submerged in peace,
The general alarm he neither hears nor sees.

The hag chaotic, in the interim,
Chanced to espy Gaudenty in his cell.
In all the monkish uproar, only him
She'd not induced with pain or bile to swell.
Frenzied, the angry hell-hound rushes in,
Hiding her treachery, by masking well

Her horrid figure, from vipers to feet
With a demeanour holy, a visage sadly sweet.

Demure and helpless suddenly she grows,
With honey coating her venomous sting;
Her head bent sadly, teary eye half-closed
(Yet with passionate fire smouldering),
Her cheeks have paled, her lips have lost their rose,
She hardly speaks, each word soliciting
A groan of woe defenceless. Thus seemed she,
Deceptive hell-hag, when she approached Gaudenty.

'You sleep, my knight, while all the rest are waking?
You're at your ease, while all your brothers weep?
Are you so lazy, selfishly forsaking
Me, and the common weal, in languorous sleep?
Arise! Your mother's heart would you be breaking?
Ingrate, her honour thus to rate so cheap!
Arise and help, if you've a beating heart!
If you're no bastard child, arise! And do your part!'

Had she not vanished as quick as she came,
She'd've caught herself a smart blow on the ear,
So quick the kindling of his soul took flame,
And he leapt from his cot, anger and fear
Racing with pity through his every vein,
So zealous to avenge his order dear.
But out the window, up into the sky
The peevish hag flew, sounding the dire battle cry.

As when Alcmene's son (so say old sages)
Set off to wrangle giants and dragon-snakes,
Seeking a hero's fame in deathless pages,
First with Nemean lion's death did slake
(And at the same time stoke) his glowing rages,
Upon his shoulders the lion's pelt did take,
Storming Gaudenty too would sure have grabbed it,
But as no pelt was handy, he took his habit.

He rushed out furious, but… he knew not whence
To battle, whom to fight… (as no foe awaited),
Calling 'To me, stout hearts! To the defence
Of our sweet mother, villainously baited!
Who fear no base foes, here! To me, my friends!
To whom the name of monk's an elevated
Title of glory, with me to the fight!
We'll show the churl how monks defend their right — with might!

It was still dark, the fiery nighttime stars
Had just begun to pale before the dawn
When the monks heard these cries of blood and wars,
Which the stone walls sent echoing on and on,
Whipping fresh terror through the corridors.
Those grouped round the old priest, like timed fawns
Spooked at the clamour nearing, all did flee,
Abandoning Honoratus to… Gaudenty.

And he too would have run, if truth be told;
He stood there trembling like a panicked child,
Poor Honoratus, but he was quite old,
You know, and soon the hero, raging wild,
Rushed on him, like mad lion in sheep fold —
But just as soon, his anger ebbed, he smiled
To see — no base-born foe, but his old friend!
And thus Gaudenty's rage came to a peaceful end.

'Father, 'tis you?' surprised, Gaudenty purred.
''Tis I,' the old man said — 'your champion!
For this my aged frame has been preserved:
To do battle against the base aspersions
Of that calumniating, vicious cur!
He's smeared our order! Sound the clarion!
Gather the novices! The time is nigh,
To crush the wretch splenetic — or with honour, die!

'Let him find out what sort of bear he's poking!
Let him find out, by harsh experience,

That when we defend our honour, we're not joking!
Let him know, we fear no man's insolence.
Let two or three more try! — Let it be spoken:
We'll beat back all their swarms, however dense!
The zeal, which guards the honour of us all,
Salves all our blessures, in our enemies' downfall.

'So now, let's hit the books!' 'The books? What for?'
Gaudenty bellowed, swollen anew with bile.
'Let weak-limbed wisemen over strophes pore,
And boast their wit, their maxims, and their style!
With fist, not feather, we'll even the score!
Let us go, as of old, to armed trial.
When stains to honour are to be redressed,
Where arm… or art, is mightier — there is righteousness!

'Wisdom and virtue — these are ancient fables,
Whose light's been snuffed out by the world refined.
Successful guile long since has turned the tables,
And victory can blanch the blackest crimes.
Who blames the underhanded, if he's able?
Who seeks support from virtue? Modern times
Cinct with the lushest chaplets of bay leaves
The brows of men called grand, for grandly they deceive.

'Let us be grand, and sly too, since we must;
Since there's no other way to win what's right,
In strength and strategy let's place our trust —
The gloomy arts that give this world its light,
Since what we deem ill wins out, since the just
And innocent are doomed to lose the fight.
Nor can we hope for miracles, my friend —
All will be well, if we but proceed like other men.'

The hag's venom was just so virulent!
Possessing with its bile Gaudenty's soul.
Honorat's hackles rose at the portent
Of such a sudden change — 'twas far from droll,

Such blasphemy! though he too was intent
On vengeance... But to reach the proper goal
By means improper? Stooping, to arise?
But then the bright new day at dawn flooded the skies.

Canto IV

Contents

The book of the War of the Monks *spreads abroad; it finds many supporters and just as many opponents. The Vicegerent predicts its defeat in a court of law; Hyacinth isn't upset at all, but Gervase is less measured in his views, and aligns himself with the confederation ranged against the author.*

> Rarely does theft ever profit the thief.
> Whatever contrary might be alleged,
> Even though it be to the public's relief,
> No euphemism, no, nor privilege
> Nor rhyme helps here: a thief's always a thief.
> No sugar coating now, no bets to hedge,
> Whether it help or harm, sicken or delight,
> Whatever the case may be, to steal's just not right.
>
> O *War of Monks!* Such your unhappy dole,
> Such a midwife assisting at your birth!
> Frivolity you from your refuge stole,
> And Curiosity cried up your worth;
> Spleen made your name from many tongues to roll
> And Fame spread you — a trifle! — throughout the earth,
> And you, of no account! Just like the spark
> That burns both hot and bright… to fizzle in the dark.
>
> Some were, who justly called you weak and lame,
> And, busied with far more important labour,
> To waste their time on such a toy disdained.
> They read you not, a waste of ink and paper.
> Others, less pompous, judge you still the same:

They'd waste no time on silly rhyming capers.
A loud, but empty noise, said they; a plot
Fantastic, silly, unworthy serious thought.

Such poets as polish their words like jewels
Thought you unworthy of their close regard;
Scholars who weigh by essence and by rule,
Scholars of sober judgement, found it hard
To see you fit for aught but village fools.
Thus, you with their generic brush they tarred:
'A graceful word-play, with a touch as light
As empty chirping, and the sense is just as slight.'

And those who care the most about the nation
Were just as valid in their quick disdain:
'How can a poem help with legislation?
Do metrical feet help bring in the grain?
Empty and useless words — below our station
To read such rot, and neither worth the pain
To write 'em. To praise 'em would be a mistake —
Far better burn 'em — with the author — at the stake.'

And yet before they toss them in the flames,
Let us return to where we left our story
(Fable, or history)… these praise, that blames;
This one is moved to laughter, that to worry;
These here are tickled, those there moan in pain…
Such is the fate of books: slander and glory.
The person of the critic is what matters:
It's bad to those it scratches, good to those it flatters.

The *War of Monks* was found on many hands
Throughout the cloister; some kept it, some scorned;
Some blessed the author, whereas others damned;
Opinion — like the book itself —was torn.
The Vicegerent an inquest would command,
And deems its legal chances as forlorn.
His better half, now loud, now still by whiles

Reading it through: grows angry, softens, weeps, and smiles.
For author, might there be an honour higher?
Hyacinth of such favour never tasted.
No one frequented her, except the prior,
But whether he did or no, he always fasted.
And if he took along with him some friar,
Such visits Hyacinth would deem as wasted.
For vain and vulgar, earthly, he thought all
Corporal delight; he tended book, not bottle.

True, he was beautiful. But is that odd?
True, he turned heads whene'er he came in sight.
Must one be ugly to serve the Lord God?
Is it a sinful thing to be polite?
Humility is lovely, is it not?
And who says holiness should not delight?
'Tis sin that is disgusting, lewd and gross;
Virtue, beauty, *to kalon* — each schoolboy knows!

Let's add good manners to the trinity.
All men should follow such a good example!
Good manners bristle not, nor harmony
With wild glare beneath its feet will trample;
It has no truck with fads or vanity,
And of suspicion's wares it will not sample.
A sweet exemplar, most averse to fight:
Father Hyacinth was both holy, and polite.

Because his interests ran to things sublime,
He knew not what was written in that book.
And when he learned of it, he'd neither time
Nor interest to even have a look.
At last he cast a glance upon the lines
That spoke of him — and no offence he took.
He neither laughed nor fumed, nor smiled, nor cried;
He yawned once, he yawned twice, and tossed the book aside.

Just as the eagle, in majestic flight
Ignores the valleys that beneath him splay,
And though it thunder, deigns not to take fright,
His eyes intent alone upon his prey
That flee before the shadow of his might,
At last, when lightning bolts around him play,
He drops his paltry harvest, swerves, and proud,
Seeks out a refuge sublime, high above the clouds.

Not of such elevated tribe was he,
Father Gervase, however reverend.
Was Hyacinth's demeanour praiseworthy?
Even so, in Gervase he would find no friend.
He'd no need of advice or piety;
He held both book and brother in contempt.
The shame and vengeance both he took to heart,
And in conspiracy resolved to do his part.

And so, determined to find still more aid,
To summon other orders, swift he flew.
But, like a watchful sentry, at the gate
He came upon Madame Dorota. True
To her name, she'd not be delayed
In urging on the work of vengeance; soon
Without e'en 'how d'ye do?' she quick relayed
With bated breath, and many a tasty frown,
All the commotion that the book stirred in the town.

He learned all that a woman's tongue might tell
Along with subtle gesture, telling glance;
With ardent breath that made her bosom swell,
And ever elegantly waving hands,
How thoroughly transmitted, and how well
The gossip — who knows one lass understands!
With mime and histrionics, variously:
Ardently, perfectly, concisely... piously.

He learned the author of the evil screed
By godless mockers had been talked around;
The lure of profit urged him to the deed
(In filthy lucre such pockets abound).
He learned how he had met with his just meed:
'He's buried in unconsecrated ground!'
How, at the crossroads, just the other night
Anna saw his soul, burning with hellfire bright.

'Thank God the rooster crowed!' 'And let him crow!'
Gerwazy roared, 'but now, I've time no more!'
And pushing past the gate, in did he go
Among the milling monks. His hopes then soared
When he heard Honoratus' cries of woe —
To nip the matter in the bud before
It grow worse yet, amidst the crowd he stands,
Coughs, and then prepares to speak, spreading wide his hands:

'O brethren! Though you're cowled in white, and though
Our habit's tan, what does that really mean?
How much we owe religious life, we know:
From it all of our common fortune springs.
United, let us march against our foe.
From tiny rivulets grow mighty streams!'
'You're right,' said Honoratus. 'Strength conjoined
Makes mighty unions. It even says so on coins.'

And so Gervase, invited to conspire
With all the zealots who would break the siege,
Into the war room with the monks retires
Where to debate on arms and strategies,
While other orders, by such zeal inspired
Swell the confederate numbers by degrees.
Then — not for vengeance at their honour's stain —
Rush in Vicegerent, Rector, with Doctor in their train.

Canto V

Contents

The assembly debates what should be done about the author. The Vicegerent, and Fathers Gaudenty, Rafał and Pankracy, are in favour of setting off to apprehend him. The Rector counsels gentler measures.

Of epic efforts are grand epics made.
Mere trifles — Trojan senate, Trojan war!
Whom, in our plight, should we approach for aid?
Should we the Muses, or Pallas, implore?
Or on Pegasus sail, with wings outsplayed?
Perhaps we'll find a clue in ancient lore,
And some old classic metricist we'll follow,
Evoking Somnus, by invoking Apollo?

So many models are there for my choosing!
Broad is the road that leads to… where I'm headed.
I do not write for fame, but for amusing
Myself, and others. There it is. I've said it.
I won't be angry if I catch you snoozing,
Dear Reader, please, snore on! And warmly bedded!
While I take up my quill and sharply hone it,
To set down for you both all I know… and do n't.

So, the cowls gathered, with biretta and cap —
And, more crucial yet, with some able heads.
The Vicegerent, a rather stormy chap
Proposed legal revenge. He stood and said,
'Well, gentlemen, we've had a nasty rap
Across one cheek; while it's still stinging red,

It's time for proper action. My advice
Is simple. I'll reveal it to you in a trice.

'That traitor, who mocks us with disrespect
Should know: his debtors we'll not long remain.
He boldly sinned, since he did not expect
Replies, and so he sits behind the screen
Of his own baseness. Now, it would reflect
Poorly upon us, slinging spleen for spleen;
It's time for court. Arrest the scoundrel firstly,
Then — unless patrician — flog him without mercy!

'What can we do if he's of noble station?
Well, let him hear my reply behind bars!
I'll see he gets… deserving arbitration,
Thump him with codices till he sees stars!
I'll find for him some nice prejudication,
And then we'll see who feathers and who tars!
With blasphemy — illegal in this land —
We'll charge him first, lumping him with the Arians.

'Even *crimen status* might be on the table:
Sought he not to embroil our lord the King
In spats with Hungary? To hands more able,
And higher placed, I'll leave such lofty things
As treason. Let each steed keep his own stable.
I'll do my bit; Lectors — to lectoring!
Quaestors, to clipping tithes from them that owes 'em,
And Father Sexton — the *vitrium gloriosum*.

'For well I know, and trust me at my word,
The scoundrel soon…' But he was prevented
From more speech by Gaudenty. 'Fine, my lord —
But such a missile will fly wide his head!
You whistle, and he'll trot here, as if spurred,
To lawsuits? Hear my remedy instead:
From our pain will the lout his mirth be taking?
I say, roll up the sleeves, and set him to aching!'

As when some lazy afternoon, a breeze
Sweeps through the woods, setting the leaves a-chatter,
The echo growing through acres of trees,
With gentle swelling strokes the ear to flatter,
So grew the murmurs through the assemblies,
Happy with how Gaudenty put the matter,
And those, who kept fanning such breaths of praise
Were those who smarted most: Rafał, Mark, and Gervase.

Of their congregation, three pillars these;
Three comforts to their brethren sad and yearning.
The first (after the usual pleasantries
Of greeting) spoke concisely, full of learning,
Beginning where the stately cedar trees
Cloak Lebanon, descending thence, and stirring
All there assembled, religious and the lay
As he along fair Jordan's banks progressed his way.

But then he spurned the earth and upward soared
So high, no eye could follow him in flight,
And nothing but his thunderous voice was heard
(He had rehearsed this well, and hit it right,)
From Aganippe seemed to flow his words,
Till the Vicegerent cried out in delight:
'Now there's a preacher! I've never heard fairer,
More elevated speech — the monk's a holy terror!'

And then discussions. All the reverend priests,
Surrounded by the younger generation
Of novices, to council then retreat,
Each wandering after his own congregation.
All shameful plotting of ambush then ceased
When, with loud, but seraphic intonation,
Pankracy's voice boomed out, begging a hearing;
Pankracy, who long the laurel wreath'd been wearing.

'How long will this barbarian heretic,
This Zoilus, who delights our fame to blot,

Strike us, and how long shall we bear his stick?
How long shall he demean the subtle Scot?
Until more churls as he group round him thick,
Waiting their turn to fleer at us, and taunt?
And this is what he aims at, certainly —
To smear, and tread us underfoot — eternally!'

'Until…?' On he'd have plunged, venting his grief,
But then a brother, at his zeal alarmed,
Reached up to warn him, tugging at his sleeve.
He thought to merely tap him on the arm,
But such a thump did Pankracy receive,
That he was quite knocked loose, content and form,
So that, though poised to cry out 'War!' 'Blood!' 'Damn!'
He sat down bewildered, and meekly as a lamb.

Then all grew silent, and the Doctor stood,
To urge the restive factions to accord.
He urged in vain; no one was in the mood
For peace — they cut his speech off in mid-word —
Even those in the back — with cries for blood.
So he was stifled, while the screeching hawks
Screeched ever louder, and echoing them, their flocks.

When hurricanes lambaste the ocean's waves,
Foaming the brine, which swells like hills around
The tiny ship sailors despair to save,
Expecting soon with her to sink and drown,
Let Neptune surface — the winds cease to rave,
The sea grows calm, the sky shrugs off its gloom:
Thus when the Rector, pounding with his fist
The table, see: The warring elements desist!

'The way I see it, my good gentlemen,
Both clerical and lay — all gathered here:
Why all this anger? What's in this book, then,
That's made you all to quake in pain and fear?
The follies of a lightweight poet's pen

Can so afflict the learned, pious ear?
And vengeance? My advice — I pray you heed it:
If it's a poorly written book, why, don't read it!

'But if it's graceful, on the other hand,
And written well, let's read it with a smile!
Another book once, by another man,
Had at the bishops. Were the good men riled?
Some laughed, though some the satire would have banned…
And time, which buries all in a short while,
Did what it always does. Now, long forgotten,
None take offence, all laugh, — if it e'er be thought on.

'And so I urge you, too. The other night
I chanced to read this book of the monks' war.
I must admit — I read it with delight.
As for the rest, I didn't ask. What for?
Poets dream sometimes when the sun is bright —
Who ever at their fancies should get sore?
He wrote about your chalice. So? I think
We ought to invite him here, and toast him with a drink!'

So said the priest, and his demeanour mild
Gave rise to gentle stirrings in their breasts.
Soft grew the eyes that'd recently rolled wild,
And the Vicegerent, who of all the rest
Had most grown frenzied, was now meek as a child.
Honoratus put all his pique to rest;
Even Gaudenty was less mobilised
To battle, when a novel wonder drew their eyes.

Canto VI

Contents

At the Rector's command, an eleven-litre jar, encrusted with thalers, is carried in, When the fathers empty it, Truth appears at the bottom. After imparting some proper warnings to those there assembled, she disappears.

What sort of marvel was't then, that directed
Further events in an un-looked for way?
What sort of sight was this, so unexpected,
That stopped all lips with so much yet to say?
A thing of good, or ill? With awe inspected
By all assembled, clerical and lay?
And how did it appear thus in the room?
The doors burst open with a loud, resounding boom.

A bardic furore had possessed the mind
Of Father Regalat, who seethed with fire
Poetic, who impiety would bind
In chains severe, crushing all vulgar ire
In rapture, when the brusque clamour behind
Him made him jump (and almost to expire)
While all the rest leapt to their startled feet,
Some too afraid to look, some half-mad to see't

(What made the noise, the cause of their alarms).
It was… a jar. Eleven litres worth
Of liquor. Cried Gaudenty: 'Drums! To arms!'
Gervase rolled up his sleeves, Pancracy (from birth
Was action-ready), to the battle warms;
The Doctor would lief sink into the earth

From shame, while the Vicegerent's angry face
Glows red; meanwhile, the Rector's jar takes pride of place.

It stood. Now, this urn wasn't such a can
As in the ancient fables might be found.
Golden it was, and like a marzipan,
But no reliefs of beasts were graven round
Its belly. Its great claim was: it was grand,
And as such it might well one's eyes astound:
Splendid of form, ancient (so say the scholars)
And brilliant round about with bas reliefs like dollars

On which were graven all our kings of old
To the delight of all the friars' eyes:
Our good kings. Happy monarchs all, and bold —
Such figures on the surface were incised.
Zygmunts and Władysławs, of whom are told
Histories, the fame of which never dies;
Such glories that a skilled engraver draws as
The seals of our Jagiellos, Piasts and Vasas.

Such was the custom of all our forefathers,
Sadness and care never possessed their minds;
Such was the custom at those feasts of theirs,
Feasts such as by excess were ne'er begrimed:
They sipped from one jar, passing it to others,
And sly deceit never spoiled them with crime.
Good, solid manners made them gay indeed —
Sipping *usque ad hilaritatem*, beer and mead.

O splendid age! When fair simplicity
Ruled where is now refinement, politesse…
Though not so brilliant in its artistry
Or bold, inventive crafting, nonetheless
They lived quite happy, in security,
Where virtue was their guide, and kindliness.
Honoured exemplars, whom no villainy taints!
God grant that our forefathers rest among the saints!

But we've neglected our krater too long.
Time to take it in hand — with meet respect,
So that it salve those hearts bruised so with wrong.
Father Zephyrin, of pious aspect,
And holy zeal, raising his voice in strong
Blame of a world where men morals neglect,
First raised it high, then all the fathers followed;
The liquor grew less and less, with each modest swallow.

The chalice had now passed through many hands.
The Vicegerent took a nice toot of it;
The Rector then, too — the author of such plans
To cast oil on the waters — took a sip;
Honoratus demurs, wavers… demands
A taste; Gaudenty took it in his grip
Enthusiastic; all who tasted praised
The wine, which grew the less the more the toasts were raised.

Now, I think they somewhat exaggerated,
Those who wrote paeans to sobriety.
Fastidiousness is often overrated,
And harmful, when it impedes our gaiety.
The good fathers knew well he had not prated
Who said 'Drink on! Until hilarity!'
And so, with such theologians to thank,
As their reverend custom was, the reverend fathers drank.

Silent, the Doctor in a corner sat.
He did not blame the rout (as it was mild)
But his presence there? Anything but that
Be known! So he hid — as well as he might.
The Rector saw him, though. What he was at
He knew. 'Why are you holding back?' he smiled,
'From jollity? No poison's in my cup,
My reverend father! Come join the fun, now. Drink up!'

So on and on the cup passed, round and round,
And all rejoiced in innocent good cheer,

And lower sank the level, down and down,
Till all could sense the happy end was near.
The Doctor sighed, drank up the rest, and found
A wonder at the jar's bottom appear!
A miracle, as through his gullet passed
The last lees of the wine — *in vino, Veritas!*

Mendacious fables of the olden times
Said: Truth lives at the bottom of a well.
(Philosophers, it seems, do not drink wine.)
And poets too — who claim their god to dwell
In Spring Castilian — water down their rhyme.
They're not of her tribe either. So, to tell
(Ahem) the truth, drunkards by far
Are closer to her, when they speak… Hence the old saw.

The Doctor, at this vision, squealed in fright,
And set the jar down whence he'd picked it up.
(With this had disappeared his will to fight…)
Gaudenty, at the Doctor's babbling, jumped:
'What? You saw Truth? You mean by mystic sight?
Or is there really something in the cup?'
'See for yourself! Peep in, and you will find
The old saying has it right: Truth is found in wine!'

Zephyrin first, magnanimous, did rise
Into the depth of the chalice to gape;
Wherefrom a bright light shone, blinding the eyes
Of all, who cringed, but dared not to escape
The light that stunned them all and mesmerised
Them so, who stood nearby (or lay prostrate).
But then dissolved the shining cloud of light,
And Truth stood before them, visible to their sight.

'Not often do I become manifest
To human eyes, though I would gladly do;
Men greet me not with gratitude, but jest —
And when I'm incarnated in my true

Form, to approach some gathering as a guest,
Though innocents are glad, the guilty rue.
Today I stand in your midst. Quick to fight
And quarrelsome, still are you worthy of my sight.

'Whence this despair? Whence your thirst for revenge?
Because of empty scribbling? Fablings vain?
Believe me, to whom no upheaval's strange,
I know the man, whom you would gladly cane.
None of your sacred order he disdains,
Nor dart at life monastic dare he aim.
In all their wit, what do his writings prove,
Save that he would correct only that, which he loves?

The weapons of wit can be harmful, snide,
But helpful too, when they're necessary.
Behind the jokes, salubrious warnings hide,
And he, who opts to employ them boldly
Deserves not to be harshly vilified,
Oppressed and insulted vengefully!
Cast off your frenzy, still your mournful moans!
You too are men: Will you cast the first stones?

'He's said he's more than ready to recall
All that he's written, and if it's amiss,
To burn it. What can one man do, when all
Are ranged against him? Why do you insist
On persecution? Is it right to brawl?
Or should you strike your bosom with your fist?
This all will pass, if it is but a smear.
But if true, change your ways!' At this, she disappeared.

END OF THE ANTIMONACHOMACHIA

THE CHOCIM WAR

Exoriare aliquis!
—Virgil

Canto I

Contents

Osman undertakes an attempt to destroy Christendom. The spirit of evil, in the guise of Mohammed, incites him to the project. It is Skinder who advises, at a council of war, to turn the sword in the direction of Poland. At Osman's command, great armies are assembled.

> By sword over-victorious, the fame
> Of that nation, which was the scourge of God,
> Spread far and wide, just like the sea of blood,
> Innocent blood, it spilled from age to age.
> Still was its zeal unchecked, unslaked its thirst
> For cruelty, proud in its might and hot
> For more renown, it sought the trembling world
> Entire to press beneath its scimitar.
> The proud Bisurman had already set
> His throne upon the grand ruins of Greece,
> Spreading his sway over so many lands,
> So many cities grinding into dust,
> His coffers swelling with the tribute pressed
> From out the conquered. At his very name
> Whole nations shivered; once proud states would quake
> With whimpering before a blow should fall.
> The proud walls of the Holy City breached,
> The daughters of Sion groaned whole centuries;
> Buildings of splendid structure fell to ruin,
> The holy sites — even that Sacred Tomb
> Which once contained both God and Man, beloved
> Of pilgrims hastening thither from afar —
> That hill, where our redemption was worked out,
> Were trod beneath a shameful pagan's heel.

Osman the warlike ruled over them all;
Osman, whose borders spread throughout the East,
Who followed in his forefathers' footsteps,
And never flagged in pursuit of grand aims,
In hopes of emulating them yet more,
Determined to exterminate the faithful.
Impious man! To think that human hand
Might undo what the hand of God hath wrought!
Such were his thoughts, and these the imps of Hell
Enflamed to fever pitch, before his eyes
Tempting him with victor's laurel crowns,
With notes triumphant caressing his ears,
The cries of wretches tuned like dulcet songs,
Roiling his lusty heart with flames undying.
In such a way, happy and graceful men
(Or so they seem, who in reality
Are troops of bandits) whole nations oppress.
Sleep, peaceful and refreshing, is unknown
In royal palaces; huts it prefers,
Spurning the presence of kings and their pomp,
Caressing humble men on beds of straw.
Though Osman's eyes grow heavy, he cannot sleep;
Though he be bedded on the softest down.
The morning star had just put out its lamp
When Osman drowsed, at last, in fitful twists.
Then he, whose great delights are sin and lies,
That spirit cast far from his Maker's face,
Stood at his bedside, within the drapes of gold
(A tribute from the Indian enslaved),
In feigned appearance, and virtue assumed.
The human voice and figure putting on
Of Mohammed, the prophet of his tribe,
'Twas thus he spoke to the sleeping warlord:
'No time is this, my son, in bedding plush
To seek a sweet repose or taste delight;
The bright glare of the dawn gladdens the sky!
The stars are hid, the sun shines in their place.
'Tis high time to appear before the hosts

Whom you are used so bravely to command;
Arise! and show them by your spry example
It is no hero's part, to loll abed;
Arise, and act, as it befits the chief
Of such a horde triumphant, such a man
To whom the weight of armour is more pleasing
Than silk and feathers, one who wakes the sun,
Surprised to see him up before it dawns.
Your men await you now on the parade ground!
Stand now before them, be to them a spur
To even greater manliness than that
Which has so elevated them already.
The field is spread before you, eagerly
Awaiting you. And fame, the great soul's food,
Cries Come! Fame summons you, to be the one
To trample Christendom beneath the feet
Of your armed legions irresistible.
Come! Spread a black shroud o'er the Christian nations,
And stain your falchion with their impious blood —
Your Turkish swords, whose very flash brings death!'
As the gigantic bison of the wilds,
Deep in black slumber on a bed of moss
Will leap up with a roar, his hackles bristling,
At the blare of a distant hunter's horn,
Snorting his nostrils, lungs pumping like bellows,
Shot through with fear, blindly stampedes away;
With such a leap did Osman his bed forsake,
Shot through with terror at the dream prophetic.
At once the camp echoes with warlike slogans
That echo back the fierce tyrant's commands —
Fell harbingers of cruel wars to come,
And weapons flash like lightning, quickly passed
From out the armouries, while officers
Pour out on the parade ground, summoning
The bold armed hosts, upon which from on high
The glowering monarch's eye will proudly fall.
Seated upon an elevated divan,
He wasted no time in imparting his will.

The fawning legions homage their proud lord,
Rejoicing in the pain he offers them.
The first then cried, 'O fortress of the faith!
Since you would raise your sword victorious
To slay the impious, in a trice the world
Shall come to know the law of our great prophet!
The fight commenced, support him with your blade;
Spread wide throughout the world his holy writ.
In slavery we shall the stubborn yoke;
While to the pliable we shall mercy show.
The farthest lands shall know our victory;
All men shall hear our all-triumphant cries,
And Rome, that once held pride of place before
All nations, shall now kneel to Istanbul.'
Amongst the first of them before the throne
Sat Skinder, he who triumphed at Cecora.
He said: 'O king of all kings on the earth,
Hear what your slave proposes, with respect.
First take revenge upon the Polish crown.
Let them first reap the harvest of their pride.
Since you began the labour, they have lost
Quite recently both general and troops
Through haughty, stubborn combat. They were led
Into the harsh fight by their chief Żołkiewski,
Who now has aged in combat; he had led
His many legions to the battlefield
With many songs of ancient martial deeds,
Blaspheming, O Mohammed, your blest name.
But you, who make the proudest men to grovel,
Did aid your faithful, and miraculous
Gave triumph over such a haughty folk.
The fearful recollection of defeat
Bewilders them with terror. It shall be
Light work to scatter the timorous shards
Of their remaining troops; they shall disperse
At the mere handsel of our bravery.
Bring down the blade that looms above their necks;
Mother and child reduce to slavery,

And should any stand firm to meet your thrust,
Cast him with scimitar into the dust.
This people, over-confident and bold,
Has heretofore escaped your puissant yoke.
They spurn your clemency, fear not your threats,
Anarchic they, who glory in disorder,
Thinking their state to stand by such misrule.
Boldly they stand against us, stubbornly.
Begin with them — the rest will fall in line
When their first ranks are seen to fall away.'
So Skinder said, and the assembled council
Anticipated their lord's will in silence.
Then he, who sits upon the faithless throne,
Osman, his wild gaze did mollify,
As sweet hope took possession of his heart,
And omens fortunate took their first steps.
He signalled pleasure at the plan conceived
And had his hosts prepare to take the field,
Adding thereunto, he would lead himself
His armies never-vanquished. At these words,
His subject hearts were filled with jollity;
Each blessing and adoring his monarch.
Their enemies seemed nothing in their eyes,
Since, in their camp, enthroned sits their king;
Since his courageous chief would undertake
The enterprise of war, no soldier fears
The shock of combat. Messengers now speed
Throughout his subject lands, calling the folk
To battle, and with joy they swell his troops:
Eyes sparkling with booty yet not won.
Not only youths, but men of age mature
Rush to the colours, every one afire
To serve his fatherland and his monarch,
And seal with blood his faith in the Koran.
There at the summit of the sultan's gate,
Fixed to a flagpole of the purest gold,
The prophet's banner waves, covered in pearls
And rich brocade. So sacred is the sight

That people dare not raise their eye to it;
With fear they read the words upon it broidered:
*There is one God, all powerful, immense,
And Mohammad is His prophet alone.*
As soon as it was seen aloft, though distant,
Loud roars of triumph rent the very skies:
The Janissaries greeted it with shrieks,
As did the Spahis, armed with splendid bows.
The very earth shook, set by echoes trembling;
The seven-tufted bunchuks tilted down
In honour; Osman too rose, bowed his head,
And then the Mufti made such an address:
'Ye faithful! Chosen from among the nations
Of all the earth, for great and holy deeds
Of jihad, faithful sons of Ishmael!
Follow the call of never dying fame!
With gladsome hearts attack your enemy!
I here announce the heavens' glad decree:
This banner of the prophet, fluttering
Aloft, will grind your foes into the dust.
And you, great ruler of all faithful nations,
Rejoice even now in the fruits of future deeds
Of valour; you shall soon see the reward
Of works gigantic, as you raise your folk
Above your beaten foes. Let the bold tremble!
Let all the world look on in wonder! Live!
Live on to see the whole world at your feet.'
At this he takes the prophet's works in hand
And reads the fables of his Al Koran.
Then, when he'd finished with such impious prayers,
He blessed, first, his proud lord, and then the knights
By name, then all the other various castes
Of men assembled there, aided in this
By myriad Santons, Molnas and Dervishes.
When these first rituals had run their course,
The Emperor returned to Tsarograd.
More than one pasha stooped on the divan
Before him prone, in superstitious awe;

Draughts of recruits rushed in from all directions,
The quickest troops arriving from the east.
The Sultan's harsh decree summoned great hosts
Which soon covered the fields round about.
Regiments drew close from demesnes far away,
To heed the orders sounding from the throne.
From where Euphrates' waters spill in flood,
Rushing between the cliffs at riverside;
From where the Tigris bears its wealthy loads
Upon the shoulders of its swift, deep currents;
From where Araxes, humming over stone
Splits the rough banks of rocky Caucasus;
From where with a large fall, the Nile renowned
Enters with slow progress to cross all Egypt,
Refreshing the whole country with rich harvests,
To join at last the sea, by seven mouths.
Amongst the clutch magnificent of lakes
Numidian, where Mauritanians live
(These last form chosen troops), with myriad crowds
Of Ethiopians, black, from fallen realms,
All these, along with Arab tribes nomadic,
Sons of the sandy waste browned by the sun,
And those from coastlines at the ocean's shore,
Unruly draftees of Fez and Algiers,
Brash youths all — with those from prophetic zones,
Mecca, Medina, with such splendid hosts
And with them, legions of volunteers too
From Lebanese deserts and Mount Carmel…
Who might retail the myriad wild throngs?
For ever more circumcised warriors draw near.
The king beheld the folk he holds in thrall,
Gazing with pleasure on the ordered ranks,
In his mind's eye, he saw his conquered foes
Panting breath his yoke, proud of the might
Of his great majesty, he rose in thought
Above the state of man, to shake the earth.

Canto II

Contents

Terror spreads through Poland at the news of the Turkish invasion. King Zygmunt calls a council. Chodkiewicz is named leader of the knightly Polish forces. Parliament is summoned. Poland undertakes preparations for the repulse of the Turks.

> She who soars wide aloft, errant, expanding
> In flight continuous around the world;
> She who broadcasts rumour everywhere
> And crowns her work in repute and advice,
> Fame, who increases all that she reports,
> Crying her items from one hundred mouths,
> Gathered her strengths, and with her usual clamour
> Set off for Poland upon speedy wing.
> The frightened ploughman ceases in mid-furrow,
> Abandoning his team still in their harness;
> The shepherd opts to flee his pleasant flock
> Rather than watch the countryside laid waste;
> Each goes in terror of catastrophe:
> Son bids farewell to father, man to wife;
> The terrified mob takes blindly to flight,
> Saving their skin, abandoning all else.
> The kingdom's borderlands depopulate
> At the mere echo of the pagan march,
> For Osman's troops are drawing ever nearer,
> Their weapons glinting angrily aloft.
> The trembling people flee for sanctuaries
> Which fill with earnest prayers and floods of tears;
> Women and children sobbing, congregation
> And priest beg the Lord God to turn aside

His anger. Aid eternal: from fierce hands
The weak You do deliver, from harsh fate;
For Fate is in Your hands. You raise the fallen —
This you have taught us often, and confirmed.
Look down upon these wretched pale figures!
To whom will You abandon them as prey?
For You have promised, though the day seem lost —
No one has ever perished trusting You.
To You the humbled people lift their cries.
Come to their aid, dear Lord, with Your sure hand;
In You they place all hope of rescue and solace,
And though a foeman's blade loom o'er their necks,
Turn but Your eye omnipotent upon
The Turk, and he shall crawl away in shame.
Thus will you wipe away our tears, and still
Our cares, O Lord of Hosts! Turn but Your eye
Upon our enemies, and they shall fade
Like shadows burned to nothing by the sun.
Still steaming was the fresh-spilt blood of heroes
That dyed the River Dniester's banks deep crimson;
Still moist the graves at Cecora, which hold
The sacred limbs that cry unto the heavens
Their death to be avenged them by the Lord.
When the sad tidings met King Zygmunt's ear,
The monarch sighed in horror, and he wept,
Lifting his eyes to heaven, whence by God's grace
His spirit was refreshed. This was that Zygmunt
Who once exchanged a kingdom for the faith —
The honour of established Christendom.
Nor did that loss, accepted for God's sake
Sadden him in the least — As God's own servant,
He found his happiness in submission,
When he returned to Poland, where he'd ruled,
To love his people, rule them as they would,
Who raised him to the throne of their free will.
In sadder kingdoms, chance enthrones the monarch,
But hap rules not a people grand and free.
As long as they respect the majesty

Of God, and humbly walk before His face,
These never shall be stained with thraldom's taint.
Free were the lips that called him to the throne;
Free were the hearts. And such fidelity
Was theirs, as elevates a worthy man,
Respecting, loving him worthy respect.
Such then was Zygmunt, of the ship of state
Most careful helmsman, keeping straight the rudder,
Despite the storm that batters mast and sides,
Maugre the waves that thunder on the deck,
Steering the craft clear of the sunken reefs
With sure and steady hand. The crew may tremble,
But he, with manly effort, tames the swells.
The guardians of the state, brave men and sure,
All elders proven, file into the hall
To aid their fatherland with faithful counsel.
Among them: shoulders that once hefted armour,
Exemplars of love sacred, patriotic;
Bearing upon their bodies scars, like medals —
Their grey hair of their head testimony
To long years rubbed thin by helm and visor,
They sat themselves in council, these great souls,
All true! Tarnowski, see: though tempests rage,
Still is your nation rich in manly arms.
You see, Zamoyski, how inspired your son
With love of country is; O worthy soul!
Indeed, all look upon their bold descendants
With pride: Firley and Fredro, Herburt, Kmit.
O, blessed father of the Jagiellons!
You too looked down upon your royal scion
Zygmunt, who occupied the Polish throne,
And knew him for your own by his great goodness.
But virtue by itself cannot keep safe
A throne from armed attack; he suffered, you
Were pained as well. So God, in His mercy,
Allowed you to glimpse the future destiny
Of your tribe. So you saw warlike Władysław
Reign o'er his fatherland in happiness;

The last descendant of the Vasa line,
Kazimierz spent his troubled reign in care,
With treasonous thanes threatening his state
And person — base conspiracy! he fought
With fate; when fate proved overstrong, adverse,
Disowning the ingrates, he took the crown
From his too noble brow. Amidst the gloom
A new light burst forth, like a flashing spark:
Another Zygmunt Poland's throne ascended,
With heart and mind both Jagiellonian.
Although he'd prove a mild, benignant father,
Still murderous hands would be raised against him,
Which providence would bat away, the Lord
Preserving him from harm. Ill times soon pass,
And once more children group around their father.
How to avert evil? Many the paths
To lessen it, should it arrive, to stand
Firm against tyrants bold, and to defend
The commonwealth. Now, when such came to pass,
Into whose hands the state's fate to entrust,
A great leader was chosen by the council —
Hetman Chodkiewicz — by acclamation.
He was a warrior whose unvanquished sword
Was known (to their cost!) by more than one foe.
In battle, he was bold and glad of heart,
Having inherited from his forefathers
Virtue and manliness. His knightly arts
Were well refined in more than one harsh school;
So was he exercised in martial skills
As to be known throughout the world a man
Among men, first among all warriors.
At the mere echo of his battlecry
The Muscovite, who had experienced
Him in ranks opposed, would swiftly turn and flee,
(Having no wish to see his blows renewed),
To where eternal snows and frosts grip hard
The earth, and darkness thick obscures the sun.
There he cowered in pits dug in the frost.

But even so, this Lord of War severe
Found him and thrashed him soundly. Chodkiewicz,
This tested knight, had but to take the field
And soon new victories were harvested.
The pagan, more than once, stood petrified
When he caught sight of his armour aflash,
And the proud Sudermanian too, the false
Usurper of the Swedish throne merely
Won bare escape to Stockholm after he'd
Been whipped with no thread left dry at Kircholm.
Into the hands of such a man, her fate
The fatherland entrusted, proud, secure
In deeds accomplished. When the heralds spread
This news throughout the land, the whole world rang
With happy echoes, sure of victory.
The Turkish arms seemed little more than gnats
When word of Chodkiewicz's election spread
Among the people; once fearful, despairing,
The Poles, trusting the Hetman, laughed down threats.
Thus, when with rumbles thick a thunderhead
Growls angrily above the fields and meadows,
Spreading alarm through the calm villages,
Hardworking ploughmen hasten to find cover.
But then a wind tears through and dissipates
The vapours dark, and with its golden ray,
The sun sends down its benison on the earth;
The ploughman takes his harness back in hand,
Hymning his thanks to God, resuming work.
Soon, envoys from the council were dismissed
To bring the Hetman news of his election,
How he is to bring succour to the land
And set his nation firm again, secure.
Letters patent calling a Parliament
Are drawn up to summon the senators —
Although the nation trusts its government
Into a king's hands, with him, from the throne,
Reigns Liberty, a check upon decrees
Which otherwise might prove too onerous,

Shining with light that blinds. In such a way
The end and reach of government is defined:
The throne its ornament, and Liberty
The baldachin above the throne. The king
Desires free subjects, a nation worthy of him:
A chosen king respecting his election.
Of three estates the nation is comprised:
Each balancing the other, with their strengths
United. First — the king upon his throne;
The senate, being freedom's guardians;
The knights too guard the nation's destiny.
When all three are united in Parliament,
What they decree together: king, knights, senate,
Such is the nation's will: through their mouth speaks
The fatherland. Before they undertake
Any action, they lift their eyes aloft:
A proper custom for a Christian land.
What aid comes without prayer? Aid must be begged
In piety, of the Lord, the nation's fortress,
The people's sure defence. And so the pastors
Gathered to raise supplication unto God.
With pious hymns the Lord God's temples ring;
The people, humbled, raise their voice in song,
Begging the Most High to avenge their wrongs.
A countless host of women and children
Help on the rituals in each church and chapel,
Entrusting their fate to prayer with pious acts.
The priests encourage them, setting an example
Of how a faithful nation, trusting God,
Sets out to wage a just war, with His aid.

Canto III

Contents

Chodkiewicz had just been wed to Princess Anna Ostrogska, when the envoys brought him the determination of King and council to take command of the knightly Polish forces. The resulting sadness of his gentle helpmeet described. The Hetman hastens off to Chocim.

> Not always are the heavens wrapped in clouds;
> From time to time the air is light and calm.
> Not always must the sailor in his course
> Measure his strengths with storm and deadly shoal;
> Advanced age offers more than toil and care.
> Amidst the flood of human life's events,
> After the fevered traffic and harsh labour,
> It's pleasant to lay on the sun-filled shore.
> Ostrogski castle! See the honoured guest
> Who enters now into your famed arcades!
> And he enters in good time. The treasure
> That you kept hidden, now do you proclaim:
> Pleasant laughter fills the air once thick
> With cries of war, and fear and woe subside;
> Love, who spreads wide his reign benevolent,
> Love, who the thickest mail penetrates,
> Subduing knight and general alike —
> Respected aim of amorous election!
> O you, who took captive the manly heart,
> Anna Ostrogska, selected love's delight,
> Anna most honoured, virtuous and sweet!
> All hearts incline to you, such is your beauty,
> But 'tis your virtue that enslaves the more.
> All that moves intellect and stirs the eye

Are found in you, together. No vile chains
And fetters are they, which bind fast your lover;
Such are the workings of the righteous heart,
That values a sweet yoke far more than freedom.
When love takes as his home the splendid soul,
Splendid the thoughts and feelings he ignites;
Love, who bestows a happy destiny,
Engendering respect allied to virtue.
Into the ancient and esteemed halls
Chodkiewicz enters; where the walls shine bright
And the high-ceilinged chambers are adorned
With taste and graceful artifice throughout —
Wherever eye should chance to fall, sculpture
And cleverly-entwined garlands of stucco
All cheer the eye with taste impeccable.
Whatever fables ever had expressed,
Art represented there: the reign of love —
How Cupid vanquished invincible heroes,
Binding their now tame sinews with his chains,
Which lay upon them lightly. Thraldom sweet!
Uprush of tears and graceful reproaches,
Love, although a traitor bringing care
And terror in his wake, was pictured there,
Ruling the world below, the gods above.
Here Jove abandons majesty in heaven,
Taking upon himself most varied shapes;
And Neptune also metamorphoses.
Apollo flees his fellows for the village;
Venus bewails the loss of her Adonis.
Danae is enriched with golden shower,
Hercules, set amidst the ranks of heaven,
Uxorious, knits at Omphale's feet.
Even he, intent on war and vicious slaughter,
Mars, whose weapons sow chaos on all hands,
Puts on the flowery chaplet, drops his arms —
His vigour stifled with his will to fight.
This is your work, treacherous son of Venus!
Your mother's triumph, Cnidian Aphrodite,

Victrix of all the gods — to Cupid's joy.
The wedding torches were already lit,
The priest stood waiting at the altar steps,
Parents and relatives, friends, passers-by
Sent out their blessings, echoed by the crowds:
Live long and happy! In concord and peace!
May the Almighty keep you in His care!
Live, honoured pair! By your fathers' example,
As in their virtues, in their happiness
Be like them! All the eyes were on the bride,
In whose heart sadness and uncertainty
Vied with her joy. Her cheeks with modesty
Were blushing, only to grow pale again,
But then she saw her parents at her side —
Her parents sweet, and stooped to kneel before them;
She has their blessing, the priest ends his prayers,
And two upright hearts are forever joined.
But no life's ever fully free of woe.
Fate seasons happiness with bitter sorrow.
Even delightful chains of married love
Suffer severe assaults of misfortune.
Amidst the cries of universal joy,
The envoys come with their entrusted news:
Command of king and senate, a Hetman's wand
In the approaching war. Immediately,
To leave all, for the fatherland's defence.
Crestfallen at the unlooked-for decree,
All gather round the Hetman, terrified,
Complaining at the harsh destiny, all,
Sorrow and pain marking sad faces round,
And bitterly complaining lips echo
The heartsore anguish, as the music fades,
And where were happy cries, now all is silence.
Anna Ostrogska! Fresh tears slip in streams
Over your gorgeous cheeks; Love, who wraps round
The heart with fetters sweet of vows eternal
Presented you at that farewell with sad,
Sad tidings; with presentiments of danger

Too real! The sweet chain-links, so newly forged
Were strained, then torn, by too cruel destiny!
He too feels pain, but overcomes his woe;
He, at whose breast these fatal darts were aimed.
He's torn away from love's caress to war;
From feasts to battle, from his conjugal bed
To harsh embraces of bloodthirsty foes.
On these his mind is fixed, although his mien
Shines gaily, unperturbed… What he is losing,
He knows too well. But virtue so obliges
The manly disposition: courage, grit.
It was not destiny caused this, but He
Who holds fate in His hand. Almighty God,
Directing all, governing all. Chodkiewicz
Hastens to where rumours of war are loud,
Setting the fear-filled citizens atremble.
He hastens there, and lifts their fainting souls
With sweet hopes of a thunderous counterthrust.
All eyes are fixed on him, and on his men,
Who bear such cheery, eager countenance.
Thus, when the burning disk of the bright sun
Pours down its rays too fiercely, and the earth
Pants bronze beneath the vicious waves of heat,
The reaper's hope, the stalks of wheat, drop fainting;
The grain cries out for rain, refreshing showers;
The herbs long for the moisture that revives;
And when it comes, to soak the dusty soil,
The ears of corn, the grasses, herbs, rejoice:
Growing proud, straight, stretching up unto the clouds.
Kamieniec — that strange work of art and nature
Defensive, can be seen now from afar.
The fortress sits high amidst rocky mountains,
The feet of which are battered by a stream
With rapids at the chosen spot, and these
Defend approach to the unvanquished walls,
Behind which fastness, long the castle's stood.
This is the fatal flaw in the bold pagan's
Plans: this fortress of the fatherland, redoubt

Of Christendom. As soon as the Hetman,
So long awaited, appeared on the horizon,
The cannon boomed in greeting; the surrounding
Earth trembled, and the cliffs in chorus sent
The echoes of the salute far and wide.
The beast that erred with silent tread the woods
Starts terrified; the elks for covert race;
The very shepherds leave their flocks in fright,
Racing with one another for the hills.
Stay! Stay! This is your saviour's signal —
'Tis your redeemer hastening in aid —
The news sends fresh hope rushing through the hearts
Of those so lately terrorised by fear.
Stay! Stay! In safety shall your flocks now graze!
Return! Your consolation now is nigh!
Grinding of teeth awaits the faithless foe,
Now that the fatherland's defender comes,
Chodkiewicz, Poland's saviour, Poland's hope.
Anna, made orphan at the painful parting,
These cries of happiness reach not your ears!
Deep sighs your constant weeping punctuate.
With sad laments, not words of love, you fill
The house where you spend days in tears and mourning.
Your beauty changes; though still marvellous,
'Tis tinged with sadness now; you wander, sole,
Uncomforted, deep in the hidden vale,
Or shaded thicket; in such wilds you find
A silent calm, where streams purl over pebbles,
And gentle breezes rock the branches. There,
Those memories of vows reciprocal
Pass through your mind; before your eyes they stand
Like carvings on the soft bark of the trees.
The wind dies down, the rill purls on more softly,
Reverberating your soft echoed moans.
When you take voice, the songbirds all grow still,
As if they gave ear to your sad descant.
When you grow silent, they take voice again,
Chirping in sadness, adding to the pain

They'd soothe in song. Alas! Now all grows quiet
Save for the echoes of your deep laments
Which fade as well, replaced by a wild stillness,
A gloomy sadness filling dale and hill.

Canto IV

Contents

The Creator of all takes mercy on Poland. He sends forth the guardian spirit of the land, increasing the manly virtues of both Hetman and troops. A catalogue of the most renowned of the Polish knights and leaders follows.

> There, where good fortune knows no alteration,
> Enriching ever with advantage new;
> Where time is marked in swiftly rolling years
> That lose at last their mortal qualities
> Of instability; there, where the earth
> Dissolves in powder, all the planets dim,
> And all their creatures show themselves as dust;
> There, He who made the cosmos with a nod,
> Set fast the feet of His eternal throne.
> The Spring of all being lacks in nothing,
> Sufficient in itself. Still measureless,
> The goodness spilt out upon all mortal things,
> The fainting and the weak; on myriads
> Of frailties, gifts innumerable rain down
> In generosity from the Almighty.
> The archangels, inhabitants of Heaven,
> Who look upon the Face of their Creator,
> Raise hymns eternally to the Most High.
> The blest elect were at this holy office
> When, of a sudden, the firmament quaked.
> They fell upon their faces, nearly fainting.
> None dared to raise his eye toward the throne
> Of endless glory, where its splendid form
> Hovered beneath the shade of wings angelic.

There, from its foot, great bolts of lightning fell,
Making the air to shiver, shaking the plains.
The Creator permitted those who fell
Prone at the great roar of His majesty
To look upon the workings of the earth
In their eternal truth, with awestruck eye.
They saw His faithful people in a rout
Scatter before the horrid scimitar;
They looked on, as with might immeasurable
Osman sought faithful Poland's destruction.
The Voice of the Almighty, which the skies
Reverberates with awe, transporting hills
And deafening the unplumbable abyss,
The Voice destructive, the life-giving Voice,
The Voice which shatters thrones unto the dust,
The Voice desired by the longing soul,
Rang out, and shaken to the core, enthralled,
They all grew still: the thrones, the powers, the saints.
Upon the streams of tears in Poland fell
The favour of the Lord; He heard the prayers
On her behalf, and soon Poland was happy.
In vain her foes threatened her with their might.
For, there, where God's regard hovers in peace,
No matter how severe the trials that fall,
Their fierce rage shall not overcome His wards.
No fierce venom will sicken them with hate
Whom God keeps safe, beneath His wings protective.
Like roaring waters, hymns of adoration
Rose from the throats of countless ranks of spirits.
Echoes of universal praise, and thanks,
Hymned by the Seraphim consumed with love,
And those, whose special care is His creation,
The angels devoted to particular service.
He, who gave earth's dominion unto man,
Placed it beneath the guardianship of angels.
He made him little less than those great spirits,
Man, created both of flesh and soul;
To him the elements all bowed down in homage.

The animals went meek at his command;
The earth, for him, was clothed in herbs and grasses,
In man God's sacred likeness recognising.
And yet man, proud, defective, would not bow
Before his Maker, and he broke his troth.
Only since then did element, earth, and beast
Rise up against the haughty criminal:
The earth, now cursed in fecund servitude
To hands cursed likewise. Then man recognised
His error. Goodness incomprehensible
Repaired what man had ruined, overproud;
And though no longer worthy intercourse
Direct, He sent angels to him for his aid.
The one whose chief care is the Polish Kingdom
Approached the fearsome throne of majesty
And spoke: 'Most high Creator! You, who order
All things, with eye unsleeping, tender care —
Without Your support, who might rest secure?
Look: trembling Poland — people, senate, king —
Place no trust in their own too feeble strength,
But hasten for shelter underneath your cloak.
O You, who by Your holy angel freed
The prophet from the lions ravenous,
Who shattered the massed armies of Chaldeans
When unto You Hezekiah cried for aid,
Order me now to make secure her borders,
Your faithful Poland.' All the Heavens shook,
As God was pleased to grant the humble suit.
Swifter than thought the spirit disappeared,
Soaring aloft into the starry rings.
Soon did he leave the ambit of the sun,
The planets, and the other worlds, behind,
Heading for earth, where he alit in Poland,
His Poland, which he fosters faithfully,
Keeping her safe with eager promptitude.
Hidden from mortal eyes, the holy sentry
Took up his post where the great Hetman stood,
Reviewing the troops that filed before his gaze.

Over his head, the angel stretched his buckler,
Heavenly armour. Though unseen by him,
The chief's heart filled with joy ineffable,
Trebling his trust in the blest covenant
Between his nation and Almighty God,
His hope a guarantee of sure success.
He stood before the massed legions of men,
A man among them. At the sight of him,
The hearts of all knew victory to be certain,
And joyful cries of ardour met his ears.
He mounted his brave steed — who knew the weight
Of him he bore — and neighed with happiness,
Pawing the sod and snorting fire, it seemed.
The soldiers heard the stallion's slogans proud
And echoed them with praise as he drew near.
What joyful storms of sound greeted the chief,
Hetman Chodkiewicz, as he paused before them,
A throng so massive! Thus in late summer,
When fields of wheat mature and turn to gold,
Their gravid stalks drooping beneath the sun,
Rolling in billows thick when a sweet breeze
Makes them to bob, he's gladdened at the sight,
The ploughman, smiling, hundredfold returns
On his hard labour reckoning. So he
Took stock of future, and heroic, bounty.
First at the head of all was Lubomirski,
Leading contingents of his countrymen.
In him the ancient clan of Srzeniawczyks
Burst into fresh bloom, gladdening Polish hearts.
Both bold and prudent, careful and effective,
He led a legion strong of chosen youths.
The fame of your great deeds shall last forever —
Spurring you on to further victories.
One glance at you, Sieniawski, and one notes
The doughty blood of heroes pulsing through
Your veins, as you in turn lead on your troops!
Your face, in battle, graceful, unperturbed;
Your hand, the author of myriad great deeds,

Honed to the battle-art by generations
Of manly ancestors. Your victories
Surprise no one acquainted with your line!
Where others end, there you begin, anew.
Then Żórawiński comes with his legions.
Many his years — but boldness undiminished;
His age, and virtue, win the respect of all.
He goes, accompanied by varied forces
Beneath the Sign of our redemption, 'Faith'
His battle-cry, to his nation's rescue,
Ardent to avenge his injured fatherland.
To him the fatherland entrusts its fate —
He, trusted Nestor to Hetman Chodkiewicz.
Sobieski comes next, trustworthy companion
In council and in labour, faithful, leading
A shining cohort. Models of rectitude
And fearlessness, they go. Splendid of mind,
He follows in the footsteps of his clan
— Famous progenitors — to where laurel crowns
Await bestowal at the hand of Virtue,
Reserved for those who seek out noble wounds,
Willing to lay their life down for their land.
He gazed upon the Chocim fields afar,
And suddenly, as if in vatic trance,
Although he knew not whence it came, this mood,
Nor could he hear with mortal ear the words
Of glory soon to echo back his fame,
Still did he pause, and listen; muse and heed
What neither eye saw, nor ear ever heard.
Although the premonitions were unclear,
Still was his bosom filled with secret joy.
This was the voice of God — insight — that leads,
Enkindling joy in hearts, father to son.
On these same fields would Jan soon overcome
Those, whom his father Jakub fought before.
O happy sire! His inheritance
Of manliness and virtue will shine clear
Before the eyes of all, proclaiming him

A knight magnificent and bold! 'Tis here
The warlord starts his long campaign of glory!
Zienowicz led his regiments up next,
Zienowicz, known for courage and good counsel,
Who gaily straps the heavy armour on
For sake of fatherland, while on his shoulders
The deeds and honours of his forefathers
Rest too. Then came Sapieha, leading men
To war; Tyszkiewicz, keen of strategy;
Equal to him in cleverness, in blood
Closely allied, bold Czartoryski came
Leading his dashing troops. And then Zawisza:
Like to the blush of glorious day at twilight,
When first the sun spills out its fading rays,
He led a troop of eager youths, accomplished,
Equal in boldness; nowhere were they bested,
This splendid band, magnificent in courage.
These led the grand Zawisza, following whom
The light, irregular cavalry boldly pranced.
At last, a wild mob of bold-hearted rogues,
From where the rushing Dniepr's waters foam
Through endless steppes, until they join the sea,
Hurtling through shoreline cliffs. Cossacks, they were,
A horde in faith unstable, but in war
None ever keener, led by an old man
(Bold he and prudent, first among their chiefs),
Petro Konasiewicz-Sahaydaczny.
And then, when all the regiments had passed
In proud parade, those led by Chief Chodkiewicz,
The warlike Hetman, joined them to encamp
In castrum glorious on Dniester's banks.
There did he hold his council of campaign
With chosen leaders under his command.
But soon enough envoys came rushing in:
The armies of the foe were nigh at hand.

Canto V

Contents

The Polish armies cross the Dniester. Lubomirski hands the mace of command to Chodkiewicz. The Turks draw near. Chodkiewicz instils ardour into his men. The battle is joined.

> Ah you, who through the gaping maw of Hell
> Escaped to bring misfortune to this world,
> Who tears the child from his mother's bosom
> And orphans sons and daughters, in despite
> Of cries for pity; deaf, unmoved by pain,
> Godless and cruel and ever-ravenous War!
> Insatiate with misery and ruin,
> Nations and states entire you extirpate.
> And now, you threatened Poland. But of old,
> He, who keeps her safe beneath His gaze,
> Almighty God, the refuge of the guiltless,
> Extends His mighty wings above her head.
> Go, gnash your teeth, frustrated, from afar!
> She does not fear your fruitless ambushes.
> In vain you rage and broadcast fright and stress;
> Greater the Lord's might is than your assaults!
> There, where boats speed over the rapid waves,
> Where careful helmsmen quake in doubt and fear
> Of currents treacherous and eddies fierce,
> A firm pontoon-bridge stretches, locking fast
> One bank with its contrary — the brave fruit
> Of cleverness and industry. Now tamed,
> The angry flood supports on its grudging back
> A route for dryshod passage, and the men,
> No longer threatened, spurn beneath their heels

The mad course of the waters. Now, therefore,
No longer threatened with final extinction,
The Fatherland stood on the riverbanks
Like Caesar at the Rubicon, and watched
The legions of her sons set off to fight,
Taking the battle to the enemy.
Along with him stood Freedom, whose defence
Was their intent as well, and holy Faith,
Whose honour and whose life they championed.
Such were the battlecries that filled the air
From throats by manly zeal animated;
There on the Dniester banks they gathered all:
Their captain at their front, awaiting the foe.
Above their Hetman, that one sent of God,
Inhabitant of Paradise, Poland's shield,
Stretched wide his wings to bank the flames yet higher
Of martial ardour natural to his soul.
Before him, waiting on his words, afire
As well, stretched thousands — farther than eye
Could see — zealous yet disciplined. Now, when
Chodkiewicz drew near, on his splendid brow
The flames that filled his heart were visible.
Great cheers erupted from the ranks united,
Greeting their warlord. Lubomirski spurred
His proud steed close. 'Twas he who, up till now
Had kept the fate of Poland in his care.
Now, as a sign of his relinquishing
Supreme command into the Hetman's hands,
In sight of all, he raised the mace of office
And gave it to Chodkiewicz, who in turn,
Eager for battle, took it graciously
With both humility and resolution.
His eyes fell on the mace and filled with tears —
Moved to the core with pride, and yet, with sorrow,
To see the relic of a dear lost friend.
That one had been a Hetman too, wide-famed,
Respected, warlike — he gripped this same mace.
In days of happiness and frequent triumphs,

He sped the victories he had foretold
Until, at last, he came to Cecora.
There, with Żółkiewski, was this mace, which now
Chodkiewicz turned over in his two hands,
Musing at the dear blood that stained it once.
After a brief pause, Lubomirski spoke:
'I place this symbol of the Fatherland
Into your hands. Poland and Lithuania,
And all their forces are at your command,
Their virtue and their manhood. United,
They would not be divided; jealousy
Here plays no part. Love of their common land
Fills all their hearts. Beneath the Knight, or Eagle,
It makes no difference. They're brothers all,
And stand to the defence of their one mother.'
Just then — like to a thunderhead that bears
A downpour boiling in its swelling breast,
With thunder and fierce flashing lightning bolts,
That louder grow the closer it draws near,
More brightly blazing as it looms, livid,
The great crowds of the infidels gave sign
Of their approach. The hills and woods resounded
Their cries cacophonous; the whole earth shook
Beneath the tread of the numberless mob,
And clouds of dust obscured the light of heaven.
The dust cleared, and at once the enemy
Was seen: unnumbered, splendid banners fluttering,
Their flags and ensigns covering the fields,
The vales and mountainsides; their arms and helms
Flashing afar, from every mountain slope,
From vale and field and every open space
The eye might reach. From many different lands
This force was gathered; differing in speech
And custom, but united in one aim,
In one force, under one chieftain supreme.
Osman nourished a firm hope — nay, was sure
Of victory; his eye surveyed the lands
Of Poland is if they were already his.

The sight of such a massive force — so many
Nations impending ruin — was frightful,
Frightful indeed, but not so to the free.
Freedom! A people used to bearing yokes,
Wicked and mean, shall never taste your fruit,
You mark of the great soul, ornament of man!
You stream forth-gushing from the spring of virtue,
From age on age the buckler of your Poles.
From you our great good fortune courses sure.
Greater than force are you; the worthy man
Who fights on your behalf will shatter yokes,
Or, if he falls, he dies as a free man.
Neither in numbers proud, nor shining bright
In ornamental carapace, they stood,
The faithful rotes, prepared to sacrifice
Their lives for Fatherland, in virtue strong,
Eager for deeds imperishing in fame,
Filled with a martial ardour for the fray.
The Hetman, rejoicing in their fighting mettle
Wasted no time to speak such words to them:
'These are the fields, my brothers, where we must
Repay our debt to God and Fatherland,
And to posterity. This is the place
Where we, defenders of the Holy Faith
Will witness to the world the manliness
And unity of our two nations linked.
Let the vile tremble! We are not afraid
To bear the wounds of honour; here we show
What love of fatherland and faith can do.
Where duty's plain, there is no need for words.
We're here to act, my brothers, not to jabber.
Come then, and eagerly, against the foe —
Who trusts in the Almighty fears no death.
O, Fatherland! As you embolden us,
Beneath your gaze, you soon shall know for sure
Whether we're true sons, or degenerates.
Whoever's Polish, follow me!' he cried,
And in a flash rushed at the infidels,

Like to a bolt that booms out suddenly.
Where is the pen to worthily describe
The impetus with which Chodkiewicz flew
Against his enemies, his men in tow?
The whistling of the darts, the flashing swords,
The horrid shouts and screams burst at once;
Plucked bowstrings hummed, steel drummed on metal plates.
The infidels with wildness brave, the Poles
By honour urged, emboldened by virtue.
The armies fought with close support despite
The widespread front, the multitudes en face;
More than one spear was shattered like a match.
The ranks of the unfaithful blushed with gore,
While the unvanquished Hetman's weapon flashed —
A model and a spur to the Christian lines.
At last the Turkish rabble cedes the field
Before Chodkiewicz's patent heroism.
Now happy cries are raised instead of plaints.
The Lord of mercy gazed upon His own,
And He, Who never will withhold His aid
From those that trust Him, though He might
Delay the cause of joy, twice over fills
The hearts of His faithful with their reward.
No one who sets his hope and trust in God
Is ever lost, at last, no matter how
Severe the trial perilous. Meanwhile
Amidst rejoicing, at the battle's end,
Word spread that Władysław, King Zygmunt's son,
Was nearing with reserves, chafing to crush
The enemies of the Holy Cross. And so
Envoys were sent to meet him on the way
With all the offices of condign respect.
By acclamation the bold Sobieski
And faithful Żórawiński were deputed.
The envoys set out with the heartfelt words
Of all their brethren, gladly, with good will,
Their loyalty unstinted to declare,
Sealed with their blood, to their beloved monarch.

Our fathers always were eager to show
The love they bore the ruling dynasty;
Though equal to his majesty in law,
Poles always cherish the blood of their kings.

Canto VI

Contents

Sobieski and Żórawiński are sent off to greet Prince Władysław as he approaches the camp with his men. Dark night surprises them in the wilds. They approach a hermit's cottage, and he inspires them with hope, narrating the events of his life.

Having received their blessing from the altar,
The envoys are dispatched by the Hetman:
'Go now, with God. Be safe.' The massed hosts
Repeat their chief's farewell. The two set off
Along a road that leads through thickets wild.
Meanwhile, the sun sends out its dying rays,
Which barely stroke the summits of the mountains.
Day fades away, and stealthy night thickens
In silence, takes possession of the earth,
Makes black the woods, the while the deaf quiet
Adds to the wilderness a dread, which grows,
As light, man's friend, abandons him at last,
With outbled twilight, deeper still the night.
Made wary by the gloomy silence round them,
Their road seems ever more uncertain, dim;
Their ears prick when the mournful breezes moan
Deep in the thickets, booming now, then fading,
While high aloft, the treetops sway, their leaves
Set murmuring, responding to the sighs
Of waterfalls, while here and there, the beasts,
The monsters of the night, begin to howl.
Just then, they saw a light amidst the trees:
A flickering candle! So they spurred their steeds
In its direction, hearts now filled with hope

After the passage of so many hours
That now — at last — they'd find a safe refuge
Where they might rest. They galloped toward the light,
The flickering light, outstripping one another.
The night began to fade as dawn drew nigh,
Sweetening the heavens with its feeble light,
Which set the eastern skies pulsing with gold
And chased the stars away to their dark bed
Beyond the sparkling ocean. Then they saw
A pleasant valley open at their feet,
Split by a chuckling brook that wound about,
Cheering the ear with its delightful purl.
The air was filled with birdsong as the sun
Arose and blushed at their rejoicing; hymns
Echoed on all hands as the daylight grew.
The heaven-reaching oaks were soaked with dew
And lowly blooms drooped, burdened with the bright
Nectar of morning; fragrance filled the breeze
Perfumed by the sweet cups with freshness brimming.
By such splendour enchanted, the men paused,
Devouring with their eyes insatiate
The morning's glory. Then, as they passed on,
Sobieski struck off from the path a bit,
Having caught sight, just off the winding way,
Of an earthen hovel, hidden in a copse
From which, as he drew near, singing was heard.
With eye intrigued he sizes up the cottage
From which, though mean, such melody emerged,
So lovely was the song he heard, the voice.
Gently, he rapped the door, and fell, at once,
To knee upon hearing an uncanny greeting:
'Come in, Sobieski.' Then the voice repeated
'Come in, in God's name!' At which, the door opened,
And an old man stood there, bidding him to rise,
With kindly greeting. So Sobieski rose,
Concerned about the fate of his companion,
But he had barely formed the words to ask
When in came Żórawiński, no less stunned

At being recognised by such a stranger,
In such a wilderness. He too fell down
Upon his knees and clasped in supplication
Those of the old man, who calmed him: 'Fear not;
I am a man like you, praise be to God.
Know that a savage horde had lain in wait
On you,' he said, 'aware of your mission.
But God, who makes unfaithful minds to falter
Saw to it that things turned out otherwise.
Redeeming you from pagan hands, He sent
Those bandits straight into our army's ambush.
So rush the unjust ever to their ruin.
Bow down then, and raise prayers of thanksgiving
To Him, who kept you safe from evil clutches.'
Again they knelt, stunned, pale with the shock,
Sending their humble thanks to God on high,
Who kept them in His care. When they had done,
With meet respect they quizzed the old hermit
About the future of the Polish crown.
'God has all things in His care,' said the monk,
'Weak, all the wicked plots of man.
Let us fall prostrate at His mighty throne —
'Tis there the books of prophecy are set.
The greatest monarchs are dust, to His eyes;
As winds make reeds bend, so His breath, the proud;
Visiting fathers' sins upon their sons;
But great, immeasurable, is His mercy, too,
The Lord most kind, who knows his own, his hosts;
He punishes and saddens, aids and cheers;
This storm shall pass. And like the fiercest gale
Oft leaves behind no trace of its passage,
So here. The thunder and lightning will cease,
And He shall pluck us out of their menacing.
But worse shall come when, greedy for advancement,
Low men will supplant their betters in glory.
But let us not lose hope. We must trust God,
Who can return all things to their first state.
He shall return —' the old man here grew silent,

Suddenly. But in their hearts a sweet hope
Remained, in silent wonder at his words,
What that unfinished oracle might portend.
Then Żórawiński, with deserved respect
Asked him, how long he bode here in the wilds?
'Sixty years, now,' the old hermit replied —
'Thus long the Lord's command bids me remain.
Much time has passed — but what are centuries
To Him who serves the Lord? A moment merely.
There was a time when vain youth misled me,
Tempting me with the world's empty delights.
I drank my full of bile at that spring,
Enslaved by the desires of the flesh,
Till all she promised proved an empty dream,
And God, in His ineffable goodness
Opened my eyes to this world's vanity
And taught me wherein lies man's true happiness.
The road you tread, I myself followed once,
For our sweet nation's sake, and I too know
What war is, and battle's ferocity.
My scars bear witness to many a wound
And sweet it is, sometimes, to think upon
How I held terror in contempt, and fought,
Chasing the bright inheritance of fame.
I feared not death.'Tis not right to fear death
When one is fighting for one's faith, one's land.
I was with Tarnowski in Wallachia,
At Obertyn, his thunderous victory;
I faced with him the massed hordes of Tartary
Who live on rapine, war and banditry.
We chased those slavers through the open steppes
To where they drive their thralls raped from their homes:
Through Budziak and Crimea, Zaporozhe —
And there showed them what Polish blades can do.
I was at Orsza with valiant Ostrogski,
Who crushed the overhaughty Muscovite;
I saw him, who once thought himself secure,
Proud in his might, fearing no punishment,

Now come to know shame, eternal abasement,
Kneeling and meekly slipping on the yoke.
Then were my eyes sated, with gratitude!
To see the Russian routed by Konstanty.
But then I ceased my worldly wandering,
Since then do I keep vigil in this cell
Where I wear nobler livery, serving God.
Death may be nearing me at any moment.
But when that moment comes, I'll close my eyes
Without fear, though forever, my last words:
"O Lord! Keep Poland safe within Your care!'"
Tears welled in the eyes of the Polish knights,
And he wept too. But then, they dried their eyes
And spent the day in happier conversation.
Invigorated by such nourishment,
The travellers retired to their beds.
But first the old man blessed them at goodnight,
And as it was his custom before sleep,
Walked out into the wilds, lifting his voice
In grateful hymns to the Almighty Father.

Canto VII

Contents

With a large force, the Turks storm the Polish redoubt. Zawisza pursues the retreating foe after they have been repulsed. He fights with Karakas, one of the Turkish chiefs, in one-on-one combat, and kills him. However, he himself falls, struck by an arrow shot from the side by Husseyn. The Polish camp in mourning following his death.

> The gracious light had just begun to dawn
> When the armed hosts could be seen from afar.
> Chodkiewicz stood upon the ramparts high,
> Assessing the enemy disposition.
> The bugles split the air with brassy din,
> Setting the troops on tense alert. Captains
> Led their divisions onto wall and bulwark
> As scout and envoy filed in with their news.
> 'Twas this: that Osman, with immeasurable mob,
> Was stealing close upon the Polish camp.
> The Hetman was ringed round with eager men,
> Chief among whom Zawisza volunteered,
> Burning with eagerness to be the first
> To fell a foe in the coming battle.
> Chodkiewicz praised his splendid fighting mettle
> But would restrain him, till the time was right.
> Then music was heard; chaotic tones and cries
> Assaulted the ears with horrid bellowing:
> Trumpets and zurnas, davuls, kettledrums
> Augmented the fierce and unmelodious yelps,
> Multiplied all the more in echoing
> From vale and forest, cliff and mountainside.
> All this blasphemed, dear Lord, Thy Holy Name!

Vaunting their might, as they marched on to war.
But God, who stands against unruly pride,
Swelling the might of the humble and just,
God, who makes happy His faithful servants,
Deigned cast a merciful eye upon the Poles.
No more are they awed by the hostile throngs
However massive; fearless, they moved forth
To meet the challenge. Chodkiewicz was first;
Near at his side, his soldiers, young and old.
At last, when all were at their battle stations,
Set in their ordered ranks to face the foe,
The cannon roared out like triumphant thunder
And shells explosive, grapeshot, filled the air.
Into this fire strode the haughty Bisurman,
With chosen Saphis, Yassirs at his side.
The air so thick with smoke and metal was,
Their swift approach was all but unnoticed
Till they were at the very battlements.
They first attacked Sapieha's doughty men,
Osman himself egging his forces on.
At his command, blindly, fiercely they flew,
Straight at the cannons belching point-blank death.
The earth itself groaned horridly and shook,
And storms of powder spent obscured the sun.
Soon to the walls siege-ladders were attached;
Deep fosses forded by the enemy,
Whose cannon, too, efficiently broke down
Bastions to tottering ruins. Famed in arms,
Sapieha fought — manliness and despair
Fuelling his courage, strengthening his arm,
While honour, and shame at being battle-bested
Filled all the Turks with an unwonted venom.
Soon was Mahomet's banner near the top
Of the crumbling battlements. Resistance flagged,
Unfaithful lips spread wide to cry 'We've won!'
When, brave and comely, Zawisza rushed in
To turn the tide. The banners down he plucked,
At which sight — spurred by his conspicuous valour —

The Dniepr troops surged on, led by the bold
Petro Konaszewicz-Sahajdaczny.
Thus, they rejoiced too soon, the haughty Turks!
Their cries triumphant and joyful now curled
To moans of horror as the blows fell thick
Upon them, as the Lisowczyks rushed in,
Repulsing the attackers. Cloaked in shame,
The Turks retreated, with the shining blade
Of conquest hovering above their napes.
Inflamed with battle-ardour through and through,
Zawisza leapt upon the fleeing hordes,
His eyes aflame with triumph as he took
Captive the colours of the pagan troops.
His sword strew death around him; on all sides
The crowds of infidels fell helplessly.
Their hearts frozen with fear, those who could run
Ran off in shameful haste, their boldness gone.
Then, at the screams of the chaotic rout
Breasting the adverse tide of deserters,
Manly Karakas spurred his own men on,
Who had been held at the woods' edge, in reserve.
Rekindling the dying embers of war,
He cried: 'I shall be slaked with blood, or soothe
My anguished heart in death! Soon they shall see,
The bold unrighteous, what my sword can do!'
'You pagan braggart!' Zawisza made answer,
'Our lads have slain far greater men that you!
If not me, then among my men you'll find
Each one a master for your silly vaunts.'
On both sides then the combat quieted
As these two set to battle, no longer
With words, but weapons. From their steeds alighting
(Which they sent off into a nearby vale),
They fell upon each other with their spears.
Comely Zawisza, with an agile feint,
Avoided Karakas's speeding dart,
And, spinning deftly on his planted heel,
With one swipe of his sword took off the head

Of his foe, crumpled suddenly a corpse.
As Karakas fell in his heavy armour
The earth resounded as if thunder-struck,
As when fierce storms thump with repeated bolts.
Ah, then Husseyn, who sped to the Turk's aid,
Pierced brave Zawisza with a poisoned dart
Shot from the side, afar, oblique, unseen.
As the wildflower, fresh with dew and bright
With colour, wilts and curls beneath the sky
When lopped by careless reaper, so did he,
Weakened, with eyes dimmed suddenly by venom,
Totter, his neck upon his white breast sagging,
His ruddy cheeks gone pale at once; his lips
Turned livid, losing for all time the smile
Which often shone there — thus Zawisza died.
Where is the pen that can describe the woe,
The mourning and despair of those who saw
The horrid event? His faithful comrades rushed
To save his dear remains, hustling them off
Into a thick wild near at hand, and there
They laid him safe in a peaceful refuge,
Hastening back at once, enraged and vengeful,
To wreak quittance upon the Turks who flew
In cowardly retreat to their fastness.
Weyher broke down in tears at the sad news,
But nothing could restrain him as he sped
Out of the battlements, his mind bent on vengeance.
He fell upon the wild bands ever thinning;
Such was the fury of the saddened troops
That Fate, which favoured so the Turks before,
Turned round, and Polish arms now took the day,
Slaying the infidels on every hand,
The fruits of victory reaping through the field.
But then Chodkiewicz, prudent, sent out men
To reign in all these raging veterans;
And they, in victory obedient,
Returned from the field to their posts.
First did they raise their thanks to the Lord God

Before retiring, as the dark night fell,
To rest — which still would not be sweet to them,
Seeing Zawisza's body borne to camp.
The whole community, leaders and men,
Went out to meet the mournful procession.
All of the Poles were sore stricken with woe,
But none more so than Zawisza's brethren.
The troop of youths stood silent by the road.
The troop of youths, who'd lost their greatest glory.
They sobbed unashamed over the hero's remains,
Cut off by fate before he'd fully bloomed.
The corpse was covered by an ornate shroud
And lain upon a bier. The path was strewn
With flowers tossed there by Zawisza's friends.
When he was borne before the altar curtains,
The woe of all was given voice in tears.
The old wept, and the young; Chodkiewicz too
Fought back a sob to speak such words above
The honoured ashes of the fallen hero:
'Boldness and virtue, and an ardent faith —
Of all these gifts our young friend was possessed.
A youth he was unsoiled by any vice,
Lacking in nothing — now with God he rests,
Sweet sacrifice to fatherland, now hid
In Heaven's tabernacle. Ah, look down,
Look down upon the tears of those you left
Behind in premature decease. But know —
Your memory shall be a spur to us,
And an example to cheer us, now sunk
In woe. Now that you've reached that haven blest,
Now that you've run your short race to its end,
O, intercede on our behalf, that God
May show His grace unto us, looking down
In mercy on your fatherland. This sword
In our hands will avenge you, ardently,
Our woes to soften, your fame to exalt.
Come then, men, swear now to avenge our loss
And so to save our nation's liberty.'

He spoke, and as he ended, from the throats
Of all erupted cries as from one man,
The slogan on the lips of all, the same,
Spreading and growing as it passed along
The massed ranks, ever swelling, ever true.
Then pickets and sentries were set about
To watch the night through as the darkness deepened.
Zawisza's bier was covered all in wreaths,
And round his sad remains, an honour guard
Kept mournful watch over their fallen friend.

Canto VIII

Contents

Osman, surprised at the brave resistance encountered, is consumed with ire. The sorcerer Omar promises to deliver him victory through his black arts, and invokes the aid of Hell. Skinder and Husseyn, on the other hand, counsel him not to place his trust in superstition, but rather in manliness. The prudence of Chodkiewicz.

> The more he placed his hope in armed strength,
> Osman the proud, trusting to might and main,
> The more he grew irate and desperate,
> Deceived, to see his haughty plans proven vain.
> At once he called anew his councillors
> Seeking their aid, fresh gambits to concoct,
> So to harass the Polish troops, subdue,
> And extirpate at last his Christian foe.
> All came at once, at his command, so great
> They feared the Turkish tyrant to displease.
> Various tactics were discussed; at last
> Some counsellor took voice, brashly advising:
> 'There is one sure way, O grand Padishah,
> To victory: Send for the sorcerer,
> Omar, and he will shift the battle's course.
> He sees into the future, and what's more,
> So potent are his spells, when he begins
> To conjure, all your foes will be confused;
> No one before your sword's blade will escape.'
> Omar arrived as soon as he was summoned
> By the fraught sultan; he swore to destroy
> The Christian ranks, consuming them with fire
> And sword. 'Soon will you see the fates relent,

And turn to favour you, my august lord.
Soon will you tread upon their necks, alive
Or dead, as you prefer. Before your throne
Heaped as a footstool, prone, by my doing.'
There, where a long vale is split by a stream
Of purest water, is an ancient wood
Of verdant trees, the wonder of all eyes,
Named Bukowina. There, eternal gloom
Is cast by ancient oaks, beeches and firs,
Whose crowns the human eye can scarcely reach.
These wilds are infamous for a defeat
Of Polish arms, when Olbracht's knights fell there.
And ever since, strange goblins haunt the place,
Seen by the terrified inhabitants
Of nearby villages. Shepherds will oft,
When spooked, run off, leaving their flocks behind,
And when a bolt from Heaven there alights,
The valleys seem to echo with the moans
Of many thousand throats in agony.
Such screams and howling sometimes meet the ear:
A horrid screeching that makes the blood congeal.
Sometimes, they seem an army's battlecries,
The clash of armour, flashing blade on blade,
Then, of a sudden, vast infernos rage
And there, amidst the flaming oaken glades
Ghosts, much too horrible for tongue to relate,
Evil things ghoulish prowl the blazing woods.
In best of times, the boughs are overslimed
With moss eternal, dark and woebegone.
No fruit hangs from these branches; no bloom blossoms;
Sere, crabbed and shrivelled are the leaves they bear;
While in their shade thrive only venomous herbs.
About lies a foul, pestilential bog
Fed by a spring that vomits bitter waters.
No pleasant zephyr ever whispers there;
No ray of sun makes jolly these dark wastes.
A plaguey mist infects the animals
Who wander there, with fatal exhalations.

There are no birds that nest in Bukowina,
And migratory flocks give it wide berth.
For should a straggler flit therein by chance,
He has a chore to struggle his way out,
Drooping, half dead, in bobbing, sickened loops.
The impious soul here entered without tremor,
So fitting was the place for him, and cries
Discordant greeted him from hellish throats,
Cheering his ears. From all sides crowded in
The ghosts and ghouls. But, with commanding geste,
He forbade closer access, and they flew,
Vanished at once, obedient to his will.
Then, evil Omar neared a chasm's lip,
A fierce cavern, a pit that plummeted
Through the most fearsome thicket, the purlieu
Of asp and viper venomous. There he set
His tools of conjury, and digging through
The mouldy graves tangled with roots of thorn,
Pulled rotting bones from out the putrid earth.
Piling them high, beside them, on the ground
He traced a circle into which he stepped.
Then he began reciting horrid spells:
Chanting them thrice in a funereal voice,
Proceeding thence to acid blasphemies
Which, as he growled on, multiplying sin
On sin, a deafening hum arose, a chaos
Of moans and screams emerging from the cave.
At last, a crash, as if a thunderbolt,
Announced the advent of the sprites of Hell.
These did the furious barbarian enmesh
Within the warp of his impious spells;
So great his evil power, that he forced
The slaves of hell to serve him, with an oath.
Thus trusting to the troth of the enslaved,
He broke his spells and freed them — for the nonce —
Hasting with confidence to Osman's side
To cheer the anxious tyrant. Him he found
Still locked in council with his chosen pashas.

Through sentries sending word of his conquests,
He was without delay admitted in,
And there he to the moot revealed his deeds.
While the bold magus' art was praised by many,
Brave Skinder from his place arose, to halt
The paeans sung to Omar's glory.
'I crave your pardon, O unvanquished Caesar,
That I cut short speech unworthy of you!
Such tricks make not a proper brace for thrones;
'Tis martial might, not words, that states enlarge.
Manliness spurns all vicious superstition.
In us, my lord, you'll find your ready succour.
If bravery can't redeem catastrophes
Late suffered, fierce despair will turn the tide.'
Then spoke Husseyn, who had barely arrived
From Baghdad's fiefdom with his massy troops
Collected from the far reaches of Persia
And the near banks of River Euphrates.
He said — 'Evil the methods, which would dim
The spotless lustre of your majesty.
Let cowards play at sorcery and sacrifice;
Glory and honour, these are manly spells.'
But Osman replied not. He made a sign
That choked discussion. Before he stepped down
From his high divan, he praised all the men
For their brave counsel, and their splendid vim;
He dispositioned all accordingly
To station held, what they ought next to do.
All did obeisance before the throne,
Retiring, as the night rolled near to dawn.
All except Omar. He remained there still
At Osman's side, enriched with the tyrant's favour
And largess, to plot more in private parley.
Chodkiewicz too was watching at that hour,
Touring the camp, the tents, the battlements,
Meticulously seeing to repairs
Of bastions battered, ever musing on
His enemy's next sally, brewing plans

To thwart the next day's thrusts. But careworn? No —
His springs of martial ardour were unfailing,
Feeding the fecund furrows of his mind,
Which gave forth to the sun new stratagems
Ensuring victory to his brave troops.
Thus does the careful sailor, as he steers
To port after a storm he's weathered through —
Although the gale winds drop, although the wind
Seems to die off, he will not trust the calm,
Whose treachery he knows. The helmsman nods,
But he, the captain, swings the boom to tack,
Gripping the rudder in his brawny fist,
Reading the winds, skirting each reef and shoal.
Then, as the gentle Zephyr, in the midst
Of swelter, when the sun too hotly burns,
Wafts in a gracious cool to panting flocks,
So were the Poles cheered by Władysław nearing —
And as each fresh envoy came speeding in,
Announcing his progress, the sore-tried strength
Of battle-wearied arms flushed full again.
Nor was this all the news they brought. Indeed,
Unhoped-for joy — behind Władysław
King Zygmunt hastened, with levée-en-masse,
Fresh troops of volunteers from every rank
Of Polish heart. So, they would see their King
Fighting along with them! How their hopes soared
At such an unexpected buttressing!
The levée-en-masse — this the final hope
When ruin looms above the fatherland.
All men rush eagerly to wounds of valour,
Stirred by their nation's dire need of defence.
The King rides at the head of chosen nobles
All set on conquest, or a glorious death.
When such volunteers rush into the field,
Glory and freedom ride along with them,
Their sure reward — the only that they seek.

Canto IX

Contents

Prince Władysław arrives with his troops. The elder Zawisza, sent from him to Chodkiewicz as an envoy, comes across his son as the remains of the latter are borne to burial. The despair of the old man, comforted by the hermit. Władysław in camp. The battle renewed, it is halted by the fall of darkness, conjured by Omar.

> To his nation's defence Władysław sped,
> Well-versed in arms and eager for the fight,
> Consumed with ardour for his fatherland.
> And as he gazed upon the field of valour,
> Where deeds of victory had been commenced,
> He spurred his steed to front the manly force
> He led, to garner his share of the glory .
> Soon was he near those plains of natural beauty
> Where River Dniester foams its speeding waves,
> Now spreading broad its current, now in rapids
> Spurting through stony banks. He sped on more,
> Nearing the place where his thirst would be slaked,
> His thirst for martial fame — he sent as envoy
> Faithful Zawisza to announce his advent,
> The fallen hero's father, who agreed
> With eagerness to ride to Chodkiewicz.
> O wretched parent! Ignorant of fate!
> O miserable man! You know not what awaits you!
> You'd spur your steed in hopes of greeting him,
> Your son, but all your hope's in vain!
> In vain you chafe at your delayed departure —
> The child you hasten toward is no more.
> At last, he leaves; midway he takes his rest

In nearby wood, when he sees from afar
A glow unusual — a torchlit train,
Wending its solemn way through the deep shades.
A fearful premonition grips his heart.
He dares not query what this scene portends,
As nearer slides the torchlit procession.
He looks from face to face of his companions;
No one can guess what's going on. He tries
To dismount from his steed, but he cannot;
His men catch him half-swooned, and help him down.
Three times he seeks to run towards the lights,
Three times he's stopped, and cannot move an inch.
Then did the mournful dirges meet his ears
As, at a snail's pace, the lanterns drew close.
Louder now sounded sobbing, moans, laments,
Further on spread the plangent echoing —
The envoy and his men stood, petrified
At this sad plainchant; then the bier was seen,
And when they could make out who lay upon it,
The wretched father knew the fallen son.
So motionless they all stood, at the sight
Of him, dry-eyed, beholding his son's corpse;
He choked back one soft moan and, casting round
His eyes confused, shivered, fell to his knees,
Then leapt up to his feet, to throw his arms
Around his cold boy. 'O my son!' he cried
His voice thick with suffering; he fainted
And said nothing more. A sad silence reigned
While such a horrid scene played out. The pain
Immeasurable struck all who looked on
With woe. The priests in tears, too, then drew close
And sought to lead the poor old man aside;
In vain — he gripped his dead son with such force
No one might pry him loose. He weeps and moans,
And lifts his tear-streaked countenance to Heaven,
Rocking his son in his embrace. Then He,
Who wipes away the tears of those in pain
And penetrates the heart's deepest recesses,

Inspired the hermit to leave his retreat,
Impelling him toward the forest glades
Where he met with the funeral conduct.
This was, he recognised, where God urged him
To be, to comfort the father comfortless.
So he approached him, with eyes full of tears,
Heart full of pity, and raised him from the ground
(Quite senseless of his presence, Zawisza,
Who pierced the hearts of all with mournful cries.)
To whom the Hermit, full of trust in God
Said, 'Rise — this vanity exceeds it mark.
Despair is the demesne of the unfaithful.
What child so wails at his father's chastening?'
The old man stiffened, pale and drowned in tears
At that voice, in which he heard the Lord speaking.
It sank into the depths of his sad heart,
Nourishing him, strengthening him anew.
It was as if scales had fallen from his eyes;
Refreshed and yet still full of wonderment
At the new brawn that firmed his sagging frame,
Such words he spoke to the holy hermit:
'Who are you? Man? Or by the will of God,
Angelic spirit sent to comfort me?
You, who by words of inspiration grand
Effect such drastic changes in my soul?
Reveal yourself, that I might meetly thank
You, and Him who sent you, praised be His name!
Are you a man like me? Or spirit blest?
Tell me, who so can shake the heart at will!'
The hermit said, 'I am a wretched man,
A worm born of the clay, who shall return
Unto it; but a vessel weak, into
Which God pours grace, to His greater glory,
By His unfettered will, to show the faithful:
His promises once given He upholds;
Who dries the tears of all of those who weep.
To Him direct your words of praise, Who wields
A rod that smarts and chastens, but Who never

Abandons to despair those Whom he tests.'
Like rain that falls on parched, cracked, thirsty soil
So were the words courageous of the hermit.
Comfort and peace soak through the old man's heart,
Moved with the grace and mercy of his God.
He bids farewell at once, and for all time,
To the vain world, opting for hermitage
Over the castle and the battlefield;
The purling of a stream through lonely cliffs
Over pomp and tinsel. But one final act
Before he changes mail for cowl: his son —
Precious remains — to the earth he returns.
Zawisza from that time serves only God,
Soothing his sorrows with sweet orisons,
Astounded, sometimes, that he'd loved the world
As much as he once did, the world that gives
Bitterness in exchange for courtship fond;
The world, that seemed a trifle now. His heart
Still ached with mourning, but in measured woe;
Each day he visits his dear child's grave
Petitioning God with hymn and earnest prayer,
Bedewing the gravemound with fervent tears.
Chodkiewicz, meanwhile, in gay martial spirit
Greets Władysław, at the head of his troops
Set for the battle and fresh laurel-harvests.
All of those armed brethren greet him too
With joy sincere that beats from all the ranks.
Cheered by the pleasant sight, Władysław swells,
And spurred by their enthusiasm, he rides
Among the regiments, who rush to war
With cheers: the battle-hardened Lisowczyks —
A fearsome cavalry! — Tyszkiewicz too,
Along with his heroic bands, who quell
The rush of the overbold spahis,
And Czartoryski, finishing the task,
Pursuing, as the spahis turn and flee.
In rushed Husseyn with his wild janissaries,
Too late to save the war-shy routed mob.

That day, Władysław did his manly part
Alongside Chodkiewicz — blood flowed in streams
(The blood of the unfaithful), and although
Skinder, confident in old victories
Resisted, long, he too soon recognised
The limits of his strength; he recognised
The end approaching of his former glory.
Filled with despair, and fretting for revenge,
The victor of Cecora rushed to battle.
Thus in the wilderness when, suddenly,
Surrounded by pikemen, the lion bold,
Encouraged by late triumphs, and enraged
At man's presumption, rushes on them
With claw and fang, nor does he sense the darts
That pierce his flanks, like matchsticks shattering
The barbed pike-shafts. See his fearsome mane
Aflutter in the wind! His horrid roars
Of conquest filling foes with shock… They waver…
Fate favoured then bold Skinder. Ziemkowicz,
Wise counsellor in senate, strong in war,
Fell, and the clouds besetting Skinder cracked
With a thin beam of hope; the infidel
Was now about to seize the warlord's banner
When, learning of his comrade's loss, the chief
Set all the might of his men there — against
The haughty potentate of janissary
And spahi. Once again the Turks took fright,
And fright soon turned to terror. Soon the blades
Of the o'ermastering Poles were poised to strike
When, catching sight of this, the sorcerer,
Omar, to shield the sultan's men from ruin,
Conjured up sudden storms and thunderbolts,
Whole trains of black clouds bearing in their wombs
The fires of lightning. All the sky was split
With furious flashes as the thunder growled.
The eyes of all were blinded by the glare
Which made the gloom but darker in dying off
Before flashing anew. The powers of Hell

We're scudding on these gales; all summoned forth
By the unholy spells. The gloom was thick
With horrid howling sounding on all sides
When hailstones fell like bullets all the while
The thunder boomed and the tornados blew.
The mountain summits seemed to be aflame
And foaming streams cascaded down their sides.
The armies, overcome by scabrous might,
Stood paralysed by fear. Their ardour cooled
With reciprocity, as no one knew
Who were their leaders, or where their mates stood —
All watched amazed in common helplessness:
Where might lie safety in such violent straits?
This was the thought that filled the mind of all
When, as with one accord, they trickled from the field.
Skinder, so close to victory through despair!
Blaspheming, in rage, cursing the sorcery
He knew to be behind this sudden turn,
Scathed the might of Hell that aided him.
Chodkiewicz was crestfallen too — rightly so,
As his the victory was, so suddenly
Stifled, wrenched from his grip. But though
Irked by the need to bend to force majeure,
Sensing that such must be the will of God,
Before Him bowing, he called back his men,
Withdrawing from the battlefield. For now.

Canto X

Contents

In dream transported to the heavenly tabernacle by the spirit of Władysław Jagiellończyk, from such heights Chodkiewicz beholds the disposition of the world, and sees the vanity of earthly things.

> Now had the horrid thunder ceased, the wind
> Died down, and in the lightning's afterglow
> The troops returned, each army to its camp
> Where they found shelter. All the chiefs inspect
> The walls and battlements to ascertain
> Whether the floods had made them insecure.
> Then, bewailing prospects suddenly dashed
> Within sight of fulfilment — in his hand!
> Chodkiewicz brooded in his lonely tent.
> Before his eyes his fatherland appeared
> Endangered, that nation he strove to aid,
> A faithful son! So, falling to his knees,
> His anxious thoughts conjoined to ardent prayer,
> He placed his trust in God, the Lord of Hosts,
> The Lord of destiny. While humbly thus
> Entreating Him, and pouring forth his thanks,
> Sleep gently crept upon him, folding him
> In grateful rest. Then to his soul God sent
> Such sights: a graceful youth of stunning beauty
> Before him stood — smiling, but who he was,
> Chodkiewicz knew not. Grasping his hand
> The youth heroic said: 'Before your eyes
> Stands Władysław, who fought for liberty,
> For holy faith and fatherland; who chased
> Illusions of vain earthly glory, and lay

His flesh, untimely, in the earth at Varna,
Slain on the battlefield before his time.
Sacred the motives were that led me there,
But savage joy beclouded my pure vows.
My penance wasn't long in coming!
I, and my army, were obliterated
By infidels. But now in sacred peace
We bide, for having lost our lives
On Christ's behalf. Thus God rewarded me,
Whom first he chastised, justly, down below,
For the impure admixture I alloyed
In soldering my pride to sacred causes.
Come now, behold!' As swift as thought they flew
To where those rest, the chosen, safe from care
And worldly misery in haven calm,
Slaked by unceasing streams of holy joy,
Calm and secure, and everlastingly
Rejoicing in bright freedom, the reward
Given them by God, Whom they see face to face.
'Many the mansions in this glorious realm,'
The spirit said, 'all won by glorious deeds.
Here happiness crowns duty and firm will,
Sweetest delight and treasure are amassed.
Great is the number of those suchly blessed
After a just life lived, their sins all purged.
Those you behold fulfilled their duty well,
And set aside their lives for land and faith.
The gift of sight now given you by God
Allows you to behold things mortal eyes
Are far too weak to bear. Look now, and see:
What splendid vistas spread before you now!
Bathed in eternal light spreading about you,
What lies before you: see in likeness, there.
What lies below you: see, perfected deeds.
What lies above — we too should strive in vain
To glimpse what God reserves but to Himself.
Behold the orbits of the stars of Heaven.
Each in its predetermined arcs and sines

Rolling majestically, ellipse and vector;
See how each star and planet in that cloud
Of worlds you mortals call the Milky Way
Speeds on, though imperceptible to eyes
Alloyed of dust and moisture, to its goal
Determined by Divine Intelligence.
Your science can't encompass this, your eye
Sees only twinklings faint, where galaxies
Sweep on at cosmic speed. And all of them
Consort together, intricately dance,
Each its own destiny fulfilling straight,
But interwoven with the others; all
From the creation of the universe
In splendid beauty hewing to God's will
In testimony visible, a sign
Of their Creator's majesty and might.
And all unfolds according to His plan —
Neither coincidence nor chance exists.
That music that you hear now, hark! The spheres
Of swiftly spinning adamant that twirl
About each other, up and down, across,
Impelled by forces various; the song
Of God's creation is what meets your ears,
A harmony that echoes evermore
In adoration of God's mighty goodness,
Day unto day uttereth speech, and night
Unto night sheweth knowledge. But look there:
That tiny speck that swings amidst the stars,
Half bathed in light, and half in darkness cloaked,
That shard — see? — which your eye can scarce make out?
That is your earth, your home by God's decree
Suspended there upon its double axis,
Between its satellites, where day by day
It sinks and rises, as His plans ordain.
Just like a pirn spun in the weaver's hand
It wraps itself in sunlight, while the moon
Follows its motions, spinning through the dark,
Whose glow, now waning, waxing full again,

Repays the earth its scot of borrowed light,
Governing tide and season by God's will.
Thence come your bumper crops, your orchards full,
The alterations of the atmosphere,
Refreshing spring, summer swelling to fall,
When ripe, the fruit of bough and glebe are gleaned,
And then, as grateful rest, the Winter comes.
The warp of swelter interweft with cool,
Rain shuttling through aridity, the web
And tapestry of life thus comes to be.
Look closer — stoop to get a better look!
See, what you take for grand upon the earth
Is shown to be a trifle, a vile jest,
Swiftly rotting, all that you deem good —
And though it shines like gold before your eyes,
How sharp, how rough the road that leads thereto!
And this you deem your happiness on earth?
Mankind can be divided in two halves,
Which — so it seems — differ in fate and fortune.
These are careworn, while those others are gay;
These have everything, those, nothing at all;
These are the humbled, those boldly command.
Two different tribes, it seems, but actually
Both king and pauper share a like wretchedness.
The wise, the simple, the wealthy, the poor —
All are subject to fortune's fickle games;
All tortured with despair and jealousy.
All suffer: these from surfeit, those from want,
Incertitude plagues every man with fear.
Go — take in hand what you will, near or far,
Whether a long life, or one swiftly flown,
It brims with sadness, pain and misery.
And truth be told, all life on earth is short
And swiftly passing, for it's but prelude,
And death, which comes to youth as well as age,
Is just to all, and plays no favourites.
Why are you loathe this exile to abandon?
Why not accept the mercy promised you?

Embrace your suffering and your toil, which lead
From earthly banishment to your true home.
Heaven is the immortal soul's homeland.
Seek to return home, holding in contempt
All passing tickles. Spurn beneath your heel
All glory bastardised. Train your heart there,
Where virtue points to everlasting fame.
Take up your arms when you return below;
The infidel will fall beneath your blows.
But be of simple mind, indifferent
To human glory; overproud in conquest
Be not, acknowledging your triumph comes
From God, who augments the weakness of men
Humble before His will. To Him give praise.
He it is sent me here to you to comfort
Your anguished mind with knowledge of His works.
You have beheld His sacred tabernacle,
The font of glory, and virtue's reward.
It's time to cast off sadness. Here behold
The place predestined you in these blest regions.
Now, praise the Lord for mercies shown to you.
Soon shall you come here…'
      Then, the vision fled,
Chodkiewicz, stunned, again fell to his knees.

Canto XI

Contents

Once again Osman leads his troops into the field, encouraging them with his presence. The brave resistance of the Poles. Chodkiewicz thunders through the field, victorious everywhere he appears. Osman flees the field. Sieniawski slays Husseyn. The Poles give praise to God for the victory.

O gracious hope! You prop of all mankind!
Although misfortunes loom like mountain ranges
On all sides, boding inexorable ruin,
Although the fatal moment be at hand,
If but your candle flicker from afar,
Man feels his strength renewed, his fainting frame
Swells mightily; vanished, his tears and moans,
He smiles, he laughs, emboldened at the sight.
'Twas you that reinforced Chodkiewicz the bold
Refreshing him with blest, stupendous vision,
Assuring him of God's favour and gifts,
Replacing bitterness with sweet. And then,
As he stepped forth into the dawning light
To battle, word came that the savage horde,
By Osman led into the field, irate
At his troops' slaughter, straining his last forces
In hopes of evening the horrid balance
By pouring on the dish the Hetman's blood,
Were drawing up in powerful battalions.
And our knights faced them, mighty in repulse.
Blasphemous were the Muslim battle-cries,
While our chief, strengthened at the Lord's table,
Trusting in God, lifted his voice in song,
As was the ancient tradition, handed down

From age to age, the massed ranks joining in
To honour the most blest Mother of God.
The Turks champed fiercely, eager, to the fray,
Venomous, snarling wildly. The whole plain
Seemed covered with their many phalanxes;
Illustrious companies, the savage clash
Anticipating hotly. All their hearts
Were filled with hope of conquest and revenge,
Waiting the signal to reprise the fight,
And it was given. Like storm clouds that swell
With thunderbolts about to be hurled down,
High above Tatra summits, growling sore
With fearsome rumblings, so the armies clashed.
Fierce shocks and savage cries were echoed back
From mountainside and wood; despair and hope
Augmenting strength of limb in the bloodbath.
Weyher, illustrious in knightly deeds,
Strongly repulsed the Arab regiments;
Weyher, respected prop of his nation,
Stood firmly there where war most fiercely swirled
About the northern quadrant of the field;
That was the epicentre, from which spilled
The most ferocious slaughter; there Sapieha
Rushed, the man chivalric, bold and mighty,
Striving to be wherever most the need.
He fought his way to where the thickest hordes
Had shown — till now — a manly resistance;
They were unmoved by the first onslaught, but
Sensing the peril of a second charge,
Where their position proved too tenuous,
In good order they drew back to the Dniester.
'Twas there that bold Husseyn planted his men
Awaiting what Destiny should next ordain.
Himself well-skilled, mature amongst the ranks
Sought out and grouped new legions in reserve.
But when he saw Sapieha turn his men
Toward him, he waited no longer, but
With eager haste he rushed upon his foe.

A cloud of dust obscured the sun, and cries
Horrid swelled through the angry clouds. Both sides
Fought boldly; iron clanged and weapons shattered,
Both armies battled with ferocity,
Led by their leaders' wit and bravery.
Into the fray first rushed those valorous
Who sought most keenly battlefield honours,
And first they were, in victory, or death.
With blood the Dniester was imbued; the heather
Was splashed with gore, the bankside rocks grew red
As the frightful quarrel raged on, and Fate
Now to this side, now to the other, inclined.
Now joyful cries would meet the ear, but then
They were drowned out by the most dreadful screams.
On this side Faith made warriors strong; on that:
A spiteful hatred made the faithless bold.
The fate of nations trembled on the scales.
Osman was seen at the head of his troops,
Ringed round by a suite of his foremost pashas,
Fierce with despair, inflamed with bitter anger,
Burning to wipe away the shame of losses
So lately suffered. When he saw the flag
Of his nemesis, there he turned his force,
Certain with overweening haughtiness
That he, and his pashas, would overcome
The armies of the faithful. At the sight
Of Osman, such a sudden cry burst forth
From pagan throats, more eager for the fight,
Crowding around him in countless numbers.
Like satellites reflecting back the glow
Of sunlight, their eyes shone with bravery
For having looked upon their lord proceeding
To his initial battle, proud, severe,
Urging his men on by word and example.
Among the regiments that circled him
A sudden screech of music then blared forth;
Blasphemous songs intoned by the imam
And echoed by the blasphemous soldiery,

Wild notes of black orisons. The banner
Of Mahomet fluttered high, splendidly,
Around which the bold pagan warriors
Pranced, with Omar behind, with sorcery
Conjuring Hell, and vowing sacrifice
Repulsive. But Chodkiewicz too caught sight
Of the unfaithful army's impetus,
And gazing at the mob immense, he cried,
'O Lord, who dost support Thy faithful always,
Have care now of the holy Christian cause!
Not our bravery, but Thy favour, Lord,
Will win the day. Trample the pagans' pride
Beneath Thy heel. For never was it known
That he who placed his trust in Thee, was lost.'
Having said this, he plunged first toward the foe.
Where'er he glanced, he heartened; where he rode,
He won, and winning, gave his men new strength.
The pagans felt again the well-known blows
Of his sabre, which blinded as it flashed;
The Turk who set out haughtily to war
Soon came to know who it was he'd provoked!
A recognition late in coming, for
It came with an abominable loss
At the hands of the avenger of Poland,
The victor who laid on a crushing defeat.
Now, there where Osman rode in gaudy pride,
In shining pomp of majesty, the Pole
Spurred on his steed, clearing his path by blade,
A shining staff of office, which drank deep
Of pagan blood, and still thirsted unslaked.
And he, who threatened all the Christian world
With haughty vaunts, now shivering and pale
Awaited not the fierce victor's approach.
No, brash Osman turned tail and basely fled.
Yes, all those tokens of Ottoman might,
The splendid banners, and gallant bunchuks,
The ranks of brave youths ripening to war,
The shining troops of noble, haughty knights,

The divers army from so many lands
Who were to spread the praise of Mahomet
Throughout the world, once we'd been trampled down,
Evaporated in swift, shameful flight.
Still fought the bold Husseyn with bravery
And vigour, proving again and again
His manly heart, achieving victories
Still, in the general catastrophe;
And when he saw his side's shameful retreat,
The disappearance of the slightest hope
Of victory, when all, quite all, was lost,
He flung himself with fury in the midst
Of swords and darts opposing. Like the sun,
When dying, pours forth its most brilliant glow,
Husseyn despairing achieved manly deeds,
Bellowing fiercely. It seemed that as he fought
He waxed the braver still, acquiring skills
Till then unknown, absorbing strength the more
He fought on, seeming to be more than man;
He fought on, searching out a worthy foil.
He found him in Sieniawski. No sooner they
Caught sight of one another than they rushed
Unto the bloody duel eagerly,
Flying unto the contest with such speed
As if they had been winged. All fighting paused
About them as the soldiers all gazed on,
Ringing them round. Their noble steeds fell first,
Making the ground slick with their blood. The men
Rose from the soil and faced each other, fierce,
In horrifying combat. All the arts
Of knightly war that have been catalogued
Were on display there, in that vicious duel.
Equal in beauty, age, and peers in honour,
In swordsmanship, in might, in grace and speed,
The bloom chivalric of their respective sides,
Their hearts brimmed equally with martial will.
At one fierce moment, all who them beheld
Acknowledged each as worthy of the other.

And many were the eyes that gazed at them,
With hope and fear shuttling through the hearts
Of all onlookers, Pole and Turk. Husseyn —
Was bold and hot to fight — but Sieniawski
Was more experienced in the arts of war.
His blade bit through the neck of his brave foe
Who, slumping sidewise, let his sabre fall,
Then, tottering to earth, fell to his knees,
Where, on his face, choking on his own blood.
Blaspheming, his vile spirit fled his flesh.
The pagans ran then, just like flitting moths
At daybreak, all those proud, disciplined troops
Ran off in scattered chaos, wide dispersed,
The shameful gaggle, by the winds of war,
The shades of evening covering their retreat
To their advantage. The faithful troops cheered
Returning to their camp rejoicing as
The nightfall put an end to that day's war.
The temple of the Lord then rang with song
As priests with hearts rejoicing lauded God
For His triumphant aid. Thanksgiving swelled
As all the congregation joined in praise
Of the Lord God, mighty and merciful.
The whole day, happy and so long desired,
Was spent in joyful celebrations, rest
At last! for the long-labouring Hetman,
And for his men exhausted with their toil.
Meanwhile, their foes, confounded in defeat,
Gazing upon the bitter fruits they won
By the presumptuous acts they undertook,
Although still breathing threats defiantly,
Within were terrified, and in despair,
Went numb with defeat. The proud ones came to learn
That numbers matter not, nor ornament,
Nor fortresses nor splendid high cities,
Nor threats and boldness are what win the day.
Their many losses made them recognise
That all their glories, faded now, were past,

Knocked to the earth by a number of men
Fewer than they, but favoured of the Lord,
Who gibed at their defeat, laughed at their shame.

Canto XII

Contents

Osman's despair. Skinder would still fight on. The Turkish army clamours for peace. Skinder, delegated to negotiate, takes his own life, rather. The death of Chodkiewicz. Seeking to take advantage of this, the Turks assault the Polish camp, but, utterly vanquished by Lubomirski, sue for peace.

There is a God, who punishes the pride
Of haughty souls, supporting His faithful.
In vain the lofty monarch threatens. More than once
Such has set flame to tinder to consume
Himself alone. For the great Lord of Hosts,
Who holds the weft of Fate in His own hands,
Is quick to aid all those who trust in Him.
The sobs of the oppressed He soon transforms
To shouts of joy. To the proud swelling flood
He set a dam unbroachable. As cliffs
Along the shore sway not in battering gales,
As sea-walls stand firm against the raging tide,
Repulsing foamy waves that froth in vain,
So His will sets a limit to all things
(Who rules the elements, rules Fate as well).
He chides the spirits of the unruly wind,
Rebukes the sea, and she is calm again.
Not might, nor numbers, helped the Turkish horde,
Whose manly spirit, undermined by pride,
By fatal vanity that like cancer spread,
Degraded was by him who overreached,
Thinking too highly of his feeble powers.
For as his blasphemies grew ever viler,
So did the Hetman's resolve grow, in step.

The manly Spirit, Who inhabits hearts
Faithful and just, tossed down the braggart proud,
And Poland once again was happy, free.
Osman, whose shame was visible to all,
Quarrelled despairing with the sullen mob.
His power, once grim, was now held in contempt,
And all around him ranged his men, near mutiny.
His moaning pashas approached the divan,
Complaining of their destiny. At this,
The imam first among the exegetes
Of Alcoran addressed the counsel thus:
'God metes good fortune to those who deserve it,
Smiting the wayward, chastising with pain
The unsubmissive. He grants victory
Not to degenerates, but to the faithful,
Who trust His laws and honour His altars.
Us has He cast down. Us, once free, He's shamed
Because of our crimes, our perversity,
Our violence. The Heavens can be appeased,
But only by repentance. Self-reform
Must stand at the beginning of each act.
Let us begin, then.' 'O, you sordid mob!'
Skinder then quashed him, 'grovelling in defeat —
The scum that barely crept into the light
From caverns where our mighty arms had chased them
Are now rejoicing in their victory?
And you would pray? The manly spirit seeks
Revenge when checked! Strong arms, not pliant knees!
O, who is used to triumph rushes out
Onto a path that leads to victory,
Or noble death!' A tumult then erupted
Among the fevered council, cries of woe
And confused echoes — a horrific roar
Of aims discordant. Osman then came in,
To learn what new proposals might be offered,
Where all now stood. The mood grew blacker still,
Mutiny threatened — a new vista, this! —
The host in terror, clamouring for peace.

The impious creature moaned, and vicious tears
Gushed from his eyes, two hot streams of despair,
And still the clamour grew. Dejected, torn,
Consumed by vengeance, vainly would he quell
The swelling insurrection fed by fear.
At last, seething with anger, pale and shaken,
He bowed his proud head. Envoys were chosen
To bear his beggar's shame unto the camp
Victorious. Among these, Skinder heard
His name indited! At which, he plunged in
The midst of all, bellowing, wild of eye:
'Let him who first encroached against the laws
Of man, himself be on his way to fix them!
Let him, whose feet erred from Submission's path
Go face his shameful sentence! He, who would
Add shame to shame by treading honour prone!
There must be some devoid of honour here
Who'll take no taint from cringing in the dust!
Let such go!' At this, he unsheathed his sword
And plunged it in his own heart. Like a crack
Of vicious thunder, so the bold man's death
Shocked all the shivering multitudes there present.
A loud groan escaped the throats of all
Seeing the great knight felled by his own hand,
Recalling all his mighty deeds of yore —
All this augmented more the pain they felt
Amidst the chaos. Thus the counsel closed,
Spahi and janissary glowering,
And peace? Who was to give it, was no more.
Yet, vain rang the echoes of the victory
Throughout the Polish camp: for the time was nigh
When even the proudest stalks of wheat must bow
Before the sickle; the time was at hand
For him, who parried all the evil blows
Of impious arms raised over his nation
His final duty to fulfil, his soul
Relinquishing in liberty to soar
To where the virtuous find eternal rest.

In tears, the warriors surround the bed
On which the Fatherland's saviour was lain.
Seeing their pain, he stirred his flagging strength,
His face pulsing once more, just like the sun
Before it sets. 'Now thank we all our God,'
He said, 'most merciful, true to His word
Given to the faithful. Let the proud tremble —
His sacred hand has smitten the mighty.
Weep not, but rather fill your hearts with joy!
Our Fatherland beloved is now secure.
She has so many faithful sons in store,
In you, if once again her praise and honour
Be challenged; she will find defenders sure,
And she will be happy. If she has weathered
So great a storm as this, that means the Lord,
The Lord of Hosts, is on her side, and though
The waves of evil threaten to engulf her,
Still will He pluck her from the dark abyss.
Always remember — hold fast to the Faith
And never waver in your devotion
To God's commandments. Be true to your kings,
Whom God establishes — never forget —
They're His anointed. And you, brothers all,
Whether grandee or humble, brothers all,
Preserve equality amongst yourselves. This is our law,
Our constitution. O, my Fatherland…!'
He died. Then, all his many virtues took
His soul in hand to lead her to the springs
Of life eternal. Thus Chodkiewicz passed.
Like to the cedar stretching heavenward,
Bathing the valleys in his cooling shade,
Immobile to the fiercest gale, he'd stood,
Sapling and shoot safe nestled in his pale,
But finally, as he was mortal too,
He sways and falls. Then, Hermon and Lebanon
Echo the mournful crash from cliff and hill.
Now, when the frightful sound came to the ears
Of the unfaithful, their resolve was firmed,

With their last strength to rush upon their foes,
Grasping the opportunity, they thought
To scour their shame now that he was no more,
Their nemesis implacable. Their moans
Once more transformed were into taunts
And they, who were so anxious to seek parley,
Now burned for vengeance, once again possessed
By that bad spirit. The alarms of war
Once more resounded as the Turkish host
Again against our bastions made assault.
Within that camp, where the Hetman's remains
Yet rested in the place of greatest honour,
Behind the rocks at riverside, the guards
Were strengthened at the battlements, and stores
To ride out sieges were amassed anew.
Bold Lubomirski, prudent, brave, worthy
To step into Chodkiewicz's role, if any,
Then took command of the army's defence.
'Twas he first breasted the wild horde's attack
When they rushed at the walls with all their might;
He, and his men, retreating not an inch,
Making the pagan flood abate. They cried,
They threatened… and their din was quelled
By Polish hearts. On all sides beaten back,
Again they felt the shame of their defeat
And in despair ferocious, fled disgraced.
You, Lubomirski, chosen on that day,
Took on the role of your nation's saviour.
By your rebuff, the Bisurman, confused,
But added to the splendour of your triumph,
In shame repulsed from bastion and rampart;
Battered by Polish arms, Polish renown
They spread as they trekked all the long road home
Defeated — Poland, defender of the innocent,
Poland, the faithful, safe beneath God's care.
Thus, those who would disseise us of our freedom
And press our necks in slavery 'neath their yoke,
Humbled anew in their renewed campaign

Were forced to sue for a disgraceful peace.
For Poland, time brought forth splendid rewards
With fame eternal won by our arms.
Undying glory to the valorous sons
Who rushed on eagles' wings to the defence
Of their blest mother! Glory evermore!

END OF THE CHOCIM WAR

GLOSSARY

The Mouseiad

I

Popiel. Legendary ruler of the Gopłanie tribe, mentioned in several mediaeval Polish chronicles The legend followed by Krasicki comes from that of Wincenty Kadłubek (XIII c.) According to him, Popiel was a weak ruler, who murdered twenty of his uncles by poison. Mice emerged from the bodies of the slain, whom Popiel refused burial, and after chasing him and his family to a tower in the lake, devoured them. These poisoned uncles are the 'forefathers' who plague the king in his drunken dream in Canto X.

Mruczysław. A comic travesty of ancient Slavic names such as Mieczysław and Władysław. Whereas those names are built from heroic roots — *miecz* meaning 'sword,' *władza* 'rule, government' and *sława*, 'glory,' Mruczysław derives from the verb *mruczeć*, or 'to meow, to purr.'

Krak. Legendary ruler of the Wiślanie tribe, founder of the city of Kraków, which is named after him.

Lech. Legendary founder of the Polish nation. Originally from Pannonia, he had two brothers, Czech and Rus, all three of whom founded Slavic states (Poland, Bohemia, Russia).

III

Homer. Krasicki makes a reference to the most famous of all mock-heroic poems, the *Batrachomyomachia*, or 'War of the Frogs and Mice,' traditionally ascribed to Homer. Most scholars are of the opinion that it arose much later, during the Hellenistic period.

Dusimyszek. Krasicki continues with the comic names. 'Gryzomir' (*Gnawer*); 'Dusimyszek' (*Mousethrottler*); 'Ruminogrobis' (*Fattychewer*); 'Gryzosław' (*Biter*); 'Miaukas' (*Meower*).

Hetman. In the old Polish-Lithuanian Commonwealth, the 'Hetman' was the highest military officer in the army. The plural of the word in English seems to be *Hetmans*, not *Hetmen*, as one might suppose.

IV
Astrea. Goddess of justice, innocence and purity. According to Ovid, as the ages declined into lawlessness, she abandoned the earth for heaven.

V
Fables. Krasicki praises the genre he is best known for.

Bajazeth. Emperor of the Turks, who is humiliated by the conqueror Tamburlaine, who keeps in him a cage. In Christopher Marlowe's play *Tamburlaine the Great*, Part I, Bajazeth commits suicide by braining himself against the bars of his cage.

VI
Astolf...Orlando. In Tasso's *Orlando Furioso*, Astolfo, an English knight, flies to Ethiopia on a hippogriff. The 'wisdom' he seeks would restore the demented Orlando to his senses.

Dulce et decorum est, pro patria mori. 'Sweet and fitting it is, to die for the fatherland.' One of the most famous quotes of the Roman poet Horace. It comes from Ode 2 of Book III of the *Odes* ('Angustam amice pauperiem pati.')

VII
Bald Mountain. A summit in the Harz Mountains of Germany, long associated with the gathering of witches. Cf. Goethe's *Faust*.

VIII
Elector of Mainz. Hatto II, Xth century Archbishop of Mainz. Like Popiel, an unpopular ruler who was also eaten alive by mice in a tower.

IX

Hercynian Forest. Forest famed in ancient lore. A German wilderness, stretching east from the Black Forest. It is often mentioned, in Caesar's *Gallic War*, for example, as an impenetrable obstacle to the advance of the Roman troops.

Sarmatian. Otherwise 'Polish.' Beginning with the Renaissance, a legend developed according to which the Polish nobility was derived from the ancient Sarmatian tribes, who fought against the Romans. With time, the word became a synonym for Poland and things Polish.

Warta. Tributary of the Oder, a river in western Poland. In this canto, it figures as the border between Germany and Poland.

Lelum Polelum. Lel and Polel are the names of supposed Slavic pagan deities. 'Lelum polelum' is a despairing supplicant's cry.

Serowind, etc. Krasicki continues with his comically appropriate nomenclature. Serosław, like Serowind, is a name based on the noun *ser* (cheese); Parmesanidas is self explanatory. Gomułkiewicz derives from *gomółka*, a sort of dried cheese comparable to Romano; Twarogus from *twaróg*, a mild, white pressed farmer's cheese, and Szperkas is probably derived from the verb *szperać* = 'to rummage around,' like a rat in search of food.

X

The catalogue of Polish kings. Lech (Xth c.) Legendary founder of the Polish kingdom. Mieszko I (died 992), first Christian ruler of Poland; Bolesław Chrobry (the Bold, 967-1025), ruler of Poland and Bohemia, Mieszko's son; Przemysław (1257-1296) died as the result of a botched kidnapping. Kazimierz III Wielki (Casimir the Great, 1310-1370), founder of the University of Kraków — Esther was his Jewish mistress, Łobzow is a section of Kraków. Jan I Olbracht ruled from 1459-1501. Stefan Batory (1533-1586); Transylvanian noble elected to the Polish throne; one of the most successful warrior kings of Poland. Władysław IV Waza (Vasa 1595-1648), of the Swedish dynasty of Vasas, the last family dynasty to rule Poland. August III (1696-1763) was the last king of Poland before Stanisław August Poniatowski, whom Krasicki leaves out of this catalogue for reasons of decorum. Krasicki's references to the drinking propensities of these monarchs is an invention of the poet's.

Kadłubek. Wincenty Kadłubek (c.1150–1223), blessed of the Catholic Church, Bishop of Kraków and chronicler. His *Historia polonica,* one of the first histories of Poland, contains both historical information as well as much mythological writing — like the story of King Popiel being devoured by mice. Written in 1774, Krasicki's *Myszeis* was composed ten years after Kadłubek's beatification by Pope Clement XIII.

MONACHOMACHIA

I
Champion of the Rosary. *Co trzykroć braci i siostry odnowił* — literally, 'who thrice re-signed the brothers and sisters' to a Sodality of the Rosary, a devotion, which the Dominicans especially promoted. There were many such pious sodalities, or brotherhoods, in Catholic Poland at the time. They centred on popular devotions such as the Rosary, the Scapular, the Sacred Heart of Jesus, and so on. It seems that Krasicki includes such barbs not out of opposition to the devotions themselves, but rather as further evidence of the monks' laziness — they don't do anything but pray. Which is, after all, the definition of the cloistered religious life.

III
The King who favours science over drinking. A nod of courtesy in the direction of Stanisław August Poniatowski, Krasicki's friend.

IV
Vicegerent or Vicesgerent. An obsolete position in the royal (not ecclesiastical) hierarchy. As the name suggests, he is a deputy of sorts, a representative of the king or the *starosta* (the district administrator).

Only one order... Possibly, a reference to the Jesuits, who were experiencing grave difficulties in connection with the temporary suppression of the order in many European lands.

Cineas. Thessalian orator prized by Pyrrhus, ruler of Epirus. Famed as a public speaker and an ambassador.

Tarnowski, Górka, Krasicki. Names of noble Polish families; Krasicki gets a chance to slide his own in!

Zoilus. Fourth century BC Cynic philosopher. Although none of his writings have survived, he had the reputation of being a vicious literary critic, speaking harshly even of Homer. For many centuries, his name was synonymous with the idea of a literary hatchet-man.

Duns Scotus (1266–1308). Scottish Franciscan. He is mostly known for his defence of the doctrine of the Immaculate Conception of the Virgin Mary. In English letters, he is important for the influence he had on the Jesuit poet Gerard Manley Hopkins (1844–1889), who derived his theory of *haecceitas* ('thisness') from Scotus' writings. Known as *doctor subtilis* ('the subtle doctor'), he was beatified by John Paul II in 1993.

Bartolus (Bartolo da Sassoferrato, 1313–1357). Mediaeval Italian jurist.

Hydaspes. River in the Indian subcontinent. A tributary of the Indus now known as the Jhelum, it was the site of an important battle between Alexander the Great and the Indian king Porus (326 BC).

ANTI-MONACHOMACHIA

II
Albert the Great (1200–1280), German Dominican priest and theologian, a commentator on the works of Aristotle. St Thomas Aquinas studied under him in Paris. Known as the *Doctor universalis*, he was canonised a saint in 1931.

Tostado (Alonso Tostado, 1410–1455). Spanish bishop and biblical exegete; he also wrote about witchcraft.

King Alfonso (Alfonso the Wise, 1221–1284). Spanish king, noteworthy for his patronage of the arts and sciences, as well as his own poetic compositions.

Fresh Recruits to the Tender-Hearted Army. A devotional work published in 1739 by the Carmelite Hilarion Fałęcki. The title gives ample testimony to its Rococo sentimentality, gently mocked here by Krasicki.

IV

To Kalon. The ancient Greek conviction that Beauty and Goodness necessarily go together.

Dorota. Another *nomen omen* in Krasicki's works. It derives from the Greek: 'Gift of God.'

Coins. A reference to the old 'red złoty' coin, bearing the phrase *Concordia res parvae crescunt* ('Little things grow by concord.')

V

Kings' medallions. Although the Polish crown quickly became an elective monarchy, three major dynasties ruled Poland throughout much of its history, and all three are represented on the large vessel. The Piast dynasty was the first, ethnically Polish line of kings. Beginning with Mieszko I in the tenth century, it died out with Kazimierz III the Great in 1370. After this, it passed into the hands of the Jagiellon dynasty, with Jadwiga's marriage to Jagiełło, the Grand Duke of Lithuania, in 1386, whose last male heir, Zygmunt II August, brought the line to a close in 1572. The Vasa dynasty, which ruled both Sweden and Poland until religious strife in the former country chased the Catholic sovereign from his throne, ruled Poland from 1587 (Zygmunt III) until 1668 (Jan II Kazimierz).

CHOCIM WAR

I

Exoriare aliquis! The motto is taken from Virgil's *Aeneid*, IV 625: *Exoriare aliquis nostris ex ossibus ultor* Literally: 'May someone arise from our ashes [bones] to avenge us!' The words are spoken by Dido just before her suicide.

Osman. Osman II (1604–1622). Turkish sultan. Assassinated after his return from Chocim by the janissaries he blamed for the defeat.

Bisurman. Outdated Polish designation for Turks, deriving from a Turkish term signifying one loyal to, or expert in, the Muslim religion.

Skinder. Iskender Pasha, Governor of Ozi. No firm dates are available for his birth, although if Krasicki is to be believed, he committed suicide in 1621.

Battle of Cecora. September-October 1620. Turkish victory over the Poles and their allies in Moldova; the Turks were lead by Iskender Pasha ('Skinder'). It was this victory that emboldened the Turks to try to expand their rule into Poland; it was this defeat that resulted in the successful defence of Chocim being seen by the Poles as vengeance for Cecora.

Stanisław Żółkiewski (1547–1620). Polish Hetman, commander of the Polish-Lithuanian army at Cecora, where he fell. Earlier, he had been successful in wars against the Swedes and the Russians, occupying Moscow for a short time in 1610.

Anarchic Poland. Because of the decentralised nature of Polish democracy, in which all nobles had voting rights and no decision could be taken without an absolute majority, the phrase *Polska nierządem stoi;* 'Poland stands by lack of government' came to be used — often as a point of pride. In Krasicki's own day and age, the Four-Year Diet (1791), which ratified the first modern constitution in Europe, tried to reform the state by, among other things, getting rid of the anachronistic, and dangerous, right of *liberum veto*.

Janissaries. Elite members of the sultan's household guard.

Spahi. Turkish cavalry.

Bunchuk. A Turkish insignia, made of decorative horse-hair fastened to the top of a staff. Often used as a field commander's staff of office.

Santons, Molnas, Dervishes. Words used interchangeably by Krasicki to indicate Muslim clergy or Islamic religious themes.

Tsarograd. Russian term for Constantinople, meaning 'city of Caesar.'

II
Zygmunt and his Swedish sacrifice. Zygmunta III Vasa inherited the Swedish throne in 1592 following the death of his father, Jan III. In order to ascend the throne, he was required to swear not to promote the re-Catholicisation of the Lutheran country, and to respect the rights of Protestants. He did so swear, and was crowned king in Uppsala, but dethroned in 1599 following a Protestant revolt. The Swedes were ready to acknowledge his son Władysław IV, but only if he were to move to Sweden and embrace Lutheranism. When these conditions were rejected, the reign of the Vasas in Sweden, and the personal union between that country and Poland, came to an end.

Jan Karol Chodkiewicz (1560–1621). Polish Hetman, widely famed in the Europe of the time for his heroic exploits in the Swedish wars. Beneath Kircholm, he achieved a stunning triumph over the enemy, conquering twelve artillery batteries and sixty Swedish standards against overwhelming odds, commanding as he did less than half of the number of troops as those opposing him.

The Polish knightly forces. Not everyone who fought at Chocim was a knight, but Krasicki constantly uses the term *Polskie rycerstwo*, in accord with his constant underscoring of the Christian army as gallant and noble, while the Turkish forces are, for the most part, described as fierce, wild, villainous.

III
Anna Alojza Ostrogska. (1600–1654). She was only twenty when she married the much older Jan Karol Chodkiewicz (who was sixty at the time). Thus, the paeans to Cupid and love that Krasicki sings here must be taken with a grain of salt.
Cnidian Aphrodite. Otherwise Aphrodite of Knidos; female nude sculpted in the IVth c. BC by Praxiteles.

Kamieniec. A fortress in Ukraine, some 30 km from Chocim.

IV

The prophet freed from the Lions. The reference is to the familiar biblical account of Daniel in the Lions' Den.

Hezekiah. In 2 Kings, Hezekiah calls upon the Lord for deliverance from the Assyrian army of Sennacherib; Jerusalem is delivered by an angel, who decimates the Assyrian troops.

Stanisław Lubomirski (1583–1649). Polish Hetman, he took over control of the Polish troops at Chocim following the death of Chodkiewicz. Here Krasicki begins a Homeric catalogue of the Polish magnate families present at the Battle of Chocim. Signal names, besides that of Lubomirski, are Czartoryski and Sapieha, but first and foremost, we have Jakub Sobieski (1590–1646), on whose diary of the battle both Krasicki and Potocki based their epics, and his son, the future King Jan III Sobieski (1629–1696) who lifted the Turkish Siege of Vienna in 1683, and who was present at the second, victorious, battle of Chocim in 1673.

Petro Konasiewicz-Sahaydaczny. (1582–1622). Cossack Hetman, responsible for introducing military discipline into the Cossack ranks.

Cossacks. A fiercely independent warlike people, famous for horsemanship, living in the south-eastern reaches of Ukraine. Krasicki considers them 'treacherous' on account of their shifting loyalty between the Polish and Russian crowns, as well as their adherence to Orthodoxy, rather than Catholicism.

V

Poland and Lithuania. The two nations had been in a personal union since the marriage of Polish queen Jadwiga with Lithuanian Grand Duke Jagiełło in 1386, and in political union since the Union of Lublin (1569).

Knight or Eagle. A reference to the insignia of the Polish and Lithuanian nations. The white eagle has been a symbol of Poland since the early middle ages. The knight, or 'rider', astride a steed with sword upraised (the so-called

Pogoń) is the symbol of Lithuania. The Polish-Lithuanian commonwealth was a federation of sorts, with certain things held in common: monetary units, foreign policy, sovereign, army, and certain powers reserved for their own territories.

VI
Władysław IV (1595–1648). Prince at the time, he ascended the Polish throne in 1632. For a short time (1610–1613) he was nominally Tsar of Russia following the successful Polish occupation of Moscow.

Wróci — 'he / she shall return.' Who this person is is anybody's guess. Perhaps a Polish monarch, returned to his rightful throne, after the restoration of the partitioned nation's independence.

Tarnowski. The hermit is speaking here of the Polish Hetman Jan Tarnowski (1488–1561), whose signal military victories he proceeds to catalogue.

VII
Lisowczyks (Lisowczycy). Polish light irregular cavalry, whose name derives from their first organiser, Aleksander Józef Lisowski (1580–1616).

Jakub Weyher (Wejher, 1609–1657) Polish nobleman of German heritage. An ardent Catholic, he was tolerant of Protestants in his lands — as his family included Lutherans as well, including a bishop.

VIII
Bukowina. Territory straddling modern-day Ukraine and Romania. Krasicki is referring to the Battle of the Koźmin Forest, where a Polish army was cut down by a Moldovan army during a botched retreat from an unsuccessful campaign launched by King Jan Olbrecht.

X
Władysław Jagiellończyk (1424–1444). King of Poland; popularly known as Władysław Warneńczyk, the appellation deriving from the place of his death, near the Bulgarian city of Varna. His body was never found; his tomb in Wawel cathedral is a cenotaph.

XI

Hymns to the Virgin. Krasicki here refers to the tradition of Polish troops singing the mediaeval hymn 'Bogurodzica' ['Mother of God'] before battle. The tradition goes back at least to the Battle of Grunwald in 1410, when Polish troops and their allies, under the command of King Władysław Jagiełło, were victorious against the German Knights of the Cross.

Molny. A building associated with an Imam.

XII

Addressed the council thus. An unclear line. The original has him addressing both the pashas and Osman: *Tak się odezwał ku radzie i panu,* if we understand the 'lord' he addresses at the end of this line as the sultan. This is confusing, since the council seems to be meeting without the presence of their lord. As the story develops, Osman enters only later, to learn of their proposed aims.

BIBLIOGRAPHY

Primary Source for the Translation

KRASICKI, Ignacy. *Dzieła poetyckie*, Vol. 1. Warsaw, 1803.

Secondary Sources

CAZIN, Paul. *Le prince-évêque de Varmie, Ignace Krasicki*. Paris: Bibliothèque polonaise, 1940.

DWORAK, Tadeusz. *Ignacy Krasicki*. Warsaw: Wiedza Powszechna, 1987.

DZWIGALA, Wanda. 'Voltaire and the Polish Enlightenment: Religious Responses,' *The Slavic and East European Review* 81/1 (January 2003):70-87.

KRASICKI, Ignacy. *Bajki. Wybór.* Warsaw: PIW, 1974.

MIŁOSZ, Czesław. *The History of Polish Literature.* Berkeley: California, 1983.

POKRZYWNIAK, Józef Tomasz. *Ignacy Krasicki.* Poznań: UWM, 2016.

SEGEL, Harold B. Review of Hoisington's translation of *Mikołaj Doświadczyński*, *The Slavic and East European Review*, 38/4 (Winter 1994): 705-706.

TARNOWSKI, Stanisław. *Historya literatury polskiej*, Vol. III. Kraków: Spółka wydawnicza polska, 1904.

ABOUT THE TRANSLATOR

Charles S. Kraszewski (b. 1962) is a poet and translator. He is the author of three volumes of original verse (*Diet of Nails; Beast; Chanameed*). Several of his translations of Polish and Czech literature have been published by Glagoslav, among which may be found: Adam Mickiewicz's *Forefathers' Eve* (2016) and *Sonnets* (2018), Zygmunt Krasiński's *Dramatic Works* (2018), four plays of Juliusz Słowacki (2018), Stanisław Wyspiański's *Acropolis: the Wawel Plays* (2017) and the complete poems and theatrical works of Tytus Czyżewski (*A Burglar of the Better Sort,* 2019). His translations of the poetry of T.S. Eliot, Robinson Jeffers, and Lawrence Ferlinghetti into Polish have appeared in the Wrocław monthly *Odra*. Recently, his English version of Jan Kochanowski's *Dismissal of the Grecian Envoys* was produced at Shakespeare's Globe Theatre in London, under the direction of James Wallace. He is a member of the Union of Polish Writers Abroad (London) and of the Association of Polish Writers (SPP, Kraków).

Acropolis – The Wawel Plays
by Stanisław Wyspiański

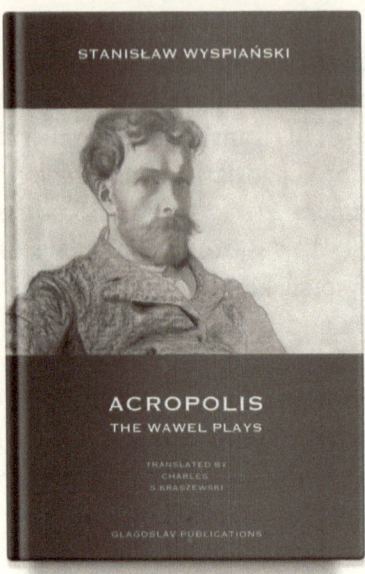

Stanisław Wyspiański (1869-1907) achieved worldwide fame, both as a painter, and Poland's greatest dramatist of the first half of the twentieth century. *Acropolis: the Wawel Plays*, brings together four of Wyspiański's most important dramatic works in a new English translation by Charles S. Kraszewski. All of the plays centre on Wawel Hill: the legendary seat of royal and ecclesiastical power in the poet's native city, the ancient capital of Poland. In these plays, Wyspiański explores the foundational myths of his nation: that of the self-sacrificial Wanda, and the struggle between King Bolesław the Bold and Bishop Stanisław Szczepanowski. In the eponymous play which brings the cycle to an end, Wyspiański carefully considers the value of myth to a nation without political autonomy, soaring in thought into an apocalyptic vision of the future. Richly illustrated with the poet's artwork, *Acropolis: the Wawel Plays* also contains Wyspiański's architectural proposal for the renovation of Wawel Hill, and a detailed critical introduction by the translator. In its plaited presentation of *Bolesław the Bold* and *Skałka*, the translation offers, for the first time, the two plays in the unified, composite format that the poet intended, but was prevented from carrying out by his untimely death.

Buy it > www.glagoslav.com

FOREFATHERS' EVE
by Adam Mickiewicz

Forefathers' Eve [*Dziady*] is a four-part dramatic work begun circa 1820 and completed in 1832 – with Part I published only after the poet's death, in 1860. The drama's title refers to *Dziady*, an ancient Slavic and Lithuanian feast commemorating the dead. This is the grand work of Polish literature, and it is one that elevates Mickiewicz to a position among the "great Europeans" such as Dante and Goethe.

With its Christian background of the Communion of the Saints, revenant spirits, and the interpenetration of the worlds of time and eternity, *Forefathers' Eve* speaks to men and women of all times and places. While it is a truly Polish work – Polish actors covet the role of Gustaw/Konrad in the same way that Anglophone actors covet that of Hamlet – it is one of the most universal works of literature written during the nineteenth century. It has been compared to Goethe's Faust – and rightfully so...

Buy it > www.glagoslav.com

Four Plays:
Mary Stuart, Kordian, Balladyna, Horsztyński

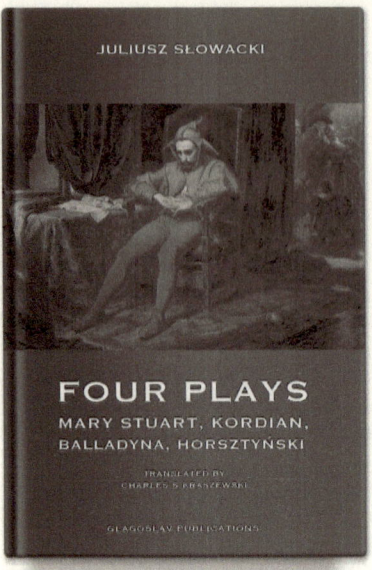

The dramas in Glagoslav's edition of *Four Plays* include some of the poet's greatest dramatic works, all written before age twenty-five: *Mary Stuart*, *Balladyna* and *Horsztyński* weave carefully crafted motifs from *King Lear*, *Macbeth*, *Hamlet* and *A Midsummer Night's Dream* in astoundingly original works, and *Kordian* — Słowacki's riposte to Mickiewicz's *Forefathers' Eve*, constitutes the final word in the revolutionary period of Polish Romanticism.

Translated into English by Charles S. Kraszewski, the *Four Plays* of Juliusz Słowacki will be of interest to aficionados of Polish Romanticism, Shakespeare, and theatre in general.

Buy it > www.glagoslav.com

MAYBE WE'RE LEAVING

by Jan Balaban

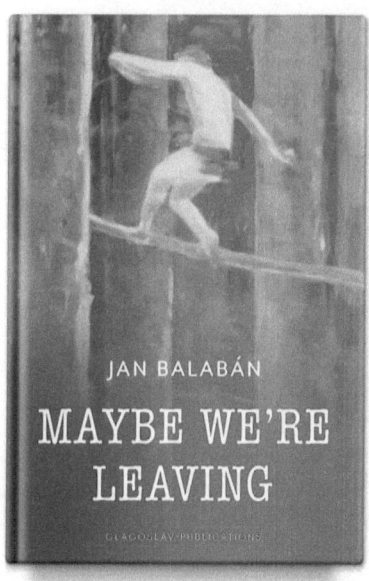

A young boy from the housing estates comes across a copse of old oaks to which he can escape, as to an oasis of calm. Although he may forget about it once he becomes an adult and "puts aside the things of childhood," it will remain a locus of balance, decades later, for a single mother struggling with the difficulties of raising the child she loves. A husband, on the lip of an ugly divorce, drives across town in the middle of the night to rescue his wife, abandoned by her lover, and then — as she falls asleep in the car — takes the long way home, to prolong a moment such as he has not experienced in years. An elderly doctor, self-diagnosed with Alzheimer's disease, makes use of the few precious moments of consciousness granted him each morning to pass on to his grandson what he has learned about life and living responsibly. Loss, and permanence, the ephemeral and the eternal, are common themes of Jan Balabán's collection of short stories *Maybe We're Leaving*, presented here in the English translation of Charles S. Kraszewski. With psychological insight that rivals the great novels of Fyodor Dostoevsky, the twenty-one linked narratives that make up the collection present us with everyday people, with everyday problems — and teach us to love and respect the former, and bear the latter.

Buy it > www.glagoslav.com

Glagoslav Publications Catalogue

- *The Time of Women* by Elena Chizhova
- *Andrei Tarkovsky: A Life on the Cross* by Lyudmila Boyadzhieva
- *Sin* by Zakhar Prilepin
- *Hardly Ever Otherwise* by Maria Matios
- *Khatyn* by Ales Adamovich
- *The Lost Button* by Irene Rozdobudko
- *Christened with Crosses* by Eduard Kochergin
- *The Vital Needs of the Dead* by Igor Sakhnovsky
- *The Sarabande of Sara's Band* by Larysa Denysenko
- *A Poet and Bin Laden* by Hamid Ismailov
- *Zo Gaat Dat in Rusland* (Dutch Edition) by Maria Konjoekova
- *Kobzar* by Taras Shevchenko
- *The Stone Bridge* by Alexander Terekhov
- *Moryak* by Lee Mandel
- *King Stakh's Wild Hunt* by Uladzimir Karatkevich
- *The Hawks of Peace* by Dmitry Rogozin
- *Harlequin's Costume* by Leonid Yuzefovich
- *Depeche Mode* by Serhii Zhadan
- *Groot Slem en Andere Verhalen* (Dutch Edition) by Leonid Andrejev
- *METRO 2033* (Dutch Edition) by Dmitry Glukhovsky
- *METRO 2034* (Dutch Edition) by Dmitry Glukhovsky
- *A Russian Story* by Eugenia Kononenko
- *Herstories, An Anthology of New Ukrainian Women Prose Writers*
- *The Battle of the Sexes Russian Style* by Nadezhda Ptushkina
- *A Book Without Photographs* by Sergey Shargunov
- *Down Among The Fishes* by Natalka Babina
- *disUNITY* by Anatoly Kudryavitsky
- *Sankya* by Zakhar Prilepin
- *Wolf Messing* by Tatiana Lungin
- *Good Stalin* by Victor Erofeyev
- *Solar Plexus* by Rustam Ibragimbekov
- *Don't Call me a Victim!* by Dina Yafasova
- *Poetin* (Dutch Edition) by Chris Hutchins and Alexander Korobko

- *A History of Belarus* by Lubov Bazan
- *Children's Fashion of the Russian Empire* by Alexander Vasiliev
- *Empire of Corruption: The Russian National Pastime* by Vladimir Soloviev
- *Heroes of the 90s: People and Money. The Modern History of Russian Capitalism* by Alexander Solovev, Vladislav Dorofeev and Valeria Bashkirova
- *Fifty Highlights from the Russian Literature* (Dutch Edition) by Maarten Tengbergen
- *Bajesvolk* (Dutch Edition) by Michail Chodorkovsky
- *Dagboek van Keizerin Alexandra* (Dutch Edition)
- *Myths about Russia* by Vladimir Medinskiy
- *Boris Yeltsin: The Decade that Shook the World* by Boris Minaev
- *A Man Of Change: A study of the political life of Boris Yeltsin*
- *Sberbank: The Rebirth of Russia's Financial Giant* by Evgeny Karasyuk
- *To Get Ukraine* by Oleksandr Shyshko
- *Asystole* by Oleg Pavlov
- *Gnedich* by Maria Rybakova
- *Marina Tsvetaeva: The Essential Poetry*
- *Multiple Personalities* by Tatyana Shcherbina
- *The Investigator* by Margarita Khemlin
- *The Exile* by Zinaida Tulub
- *Leo Tolstoy: Flight from Paradise* by Pavel Basinsky
- *Moscow in the 1930* by Natalia Gromova
- *Laurus* (Dutch edition) by Evgenij Vodolazkin
- *Prisoner* by Anna Nemzer
- *The Crime of Chernobyl: The Nuclear Goulag* by Wladimir Tchertkoff
- *Alpine Ballad* by Vasil Bykau
- *The Complete Correspondence of Hryhory Skovoroda*
- *The Tale of Aypi* by Ak Welsapar
- *Selected Poems* by Lydia Grigorieva
- *The Fantastic Worlds of Yuri Vynnychuk*
- *The Garden of Divine Songs and Collected Poetry of Hryhory Skovoroda*
- *Adventures in the Slavic Kitchen: A Book of Essays with Recipes* by Igor Klekh
- *Seven Signs of the Lion* by Michael M. Naydan

- *Forefathers' Eve* by Adam Mickiewicz
- *One-Two* by Igor Eliseev
- *Girls, be Good* by Bojan Babić
- *Time of the Octopus* by Anatoly Kucherena
- *The Grand Harmony* by Bohdan Ihor Antonych
- *The Selected Lyric Poetry Of Maksym Rylsky*
- *The Shining Light* by Galymkair Mutanov
- *The Frontier: 28 Contemporary Ukrainian Poets - An Anthology*
- *Acropolis: The Wawel Plays* by Stanisław Wyspiański
- *Contours of the City* by Attyla Mohylny
- *Conversations Before Silence: The Selected Poetry of Oles Ilchenko*
- *The Secret History of my Sojourn in Russia* by Jaroslav Hašek
- *Mirror Sand: An Anthology of Russian Short Poems*
- *Maybe We're Leaving* by Jan Balaban
- *Death of the Snake Catcher* by Ak Welsapar
- *A Brown Man in Russia* by Vijay Menon
- *Hard Times* by Ostap Vyshnia
- *The Flying Dutchman* by Anatoly Kudryavitsky
- *Nikolai Gumilev's Africa* by Nikolai Gumilev
- *Combustions* by Srđan Srdić
- *The Sonnets* by Adam Mickiewicz
- *Dramatic Works* by Zygmunt Krasiński
- *Four Plays* by Juliusz Słowacki
- *Little Zinnobers* by Elena Chizhova
- *We Are Building Capitalism! Moscow in Transition 1992-1997* by Robert Stephenson
- *The Nuremberg Trials* by Alexander Zvyagintsev
- *The Hemingway Game* by Evgeni Grishkovets
- *A Flame Out at Sea* by Dmitry Novikov
- *Jesus' Cat* by Grig
- *Want a Baby and Other Plays* by Sergei Tretyakov
- *Mikhail Bulgakov: The Life and Times* by Marietta Chudakova
- *Leonardo's Handwriting* by Dina Rubina
- *A Burglar of the Better Sort* by Tytus Czyżewski
- *The Mouseiad and other Mock Epics* by Ignacy Krasicki
- *Ravens before Noah* by Susanna Harutyunyan

- *An English Queen and Stalingrad* by Natalia Kulishenko
- *Point Zero* by Narek Malian
- *Absolute Zero* by Artem Chekh
- *Olanda* by Rafał Wojasiński
- *Robinsons* by Aram Pachyan
- *The Monastery* by Zakhar Prilepin
- *The Selected Poetry of Bohdan Rubchak: Songs of Love, Songs of Death, Songs of the Moon*
- *Mebet* by Alexander Grigorenko
- *The Orchestra* by Vladimir Gonik
- *Everyday Stories* by Mima Mihajlović
- *Slavdom* by Ľudovít Štúr
- *The Code of Civilization* by Vyacheslav Nikonov
- *Where Was the Angel Going?* by Jan Balaban
- *De Zwarte Kip* (Dutch Edition) by Antoni Pogorelski
- *Głosy / Voices* by Jan Polkowski
- *Sergei Tretyakov: A Revolutionary Writer in Stalin's Russia* by Robert Leach
- *Opstand* (Dutch Edition) by Władysław Reymont
- *Dramatic Works* by Cyprian Kamil Norwid
- *Children's First Book of Chess* by Natalie Shevando and Matthew McMillion
- *Precursor* by Vasyl Shevchuk
- *The Vow: A Requiem for the Fifties* by Jiří Kratochvil
- *De Bibliothecaris* (Dutch edition) by Mikhail Jelizarov
- *Subterranean Fire* by Natalka Bilotserkivets
- *Vladimir Vysotsky: Selected Works*
- *Behind the Silk Curtain* by Gulistan Khamzayeva
- *The Village Teacher and Other Stories* by Theodore Odrach
- *Duel* by Borys Antonenko-Davydovych
- *War Poems* by Alexander Korotko
- *Ballads and Romances* by Adam Mickiewicz
- *The Revolt of the Animals* by Wladyslaw Reymont
- *Poems about my Psychiatrist* by Andrzej Kotański
- *Someone Else's Life* by Elena Dolgopyat
- *Liza's Waterfall: The hidden story of a Russian feminist* by Pavel Basinsky
- *Biography of Sergei Prokofiev* by Igor Vichnevetsky

More coming...

GLAGOSLAV PUBLICATIONS
www.glagoslav.com

www.ingramcontent.com/pod-product-compliance
Lightning Source LLC
Chambersburg PA
CBHW031103080526
44587CB00011B/804